Power Maths

Year 4 Textbook

Series Editor: Tony Staneff

C000212778

Ash

Ash is curious.

He explores new ideas to solve puzzles.

flexible

Flo

brave

Astrid

determined

helpful

Dexter

Sparks

Pearson

Contents

This tells you which page you need.

Are you ready for some more maths?

How to use this book

These pages make sure we are ready for the unit ahead. Find out what we will be learning and brush up on your skills.

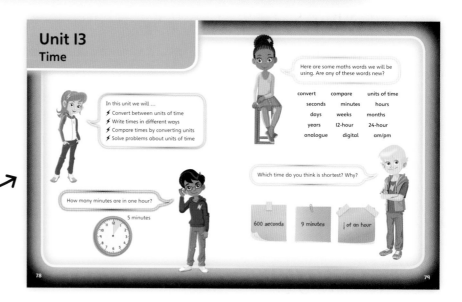

Discover

Lessons start with **Discover**.

Here, we explore new maths problems.

Can you work out how to find the answer?

Do not be afraid to make mistakes. Learn from them and try again!

Share

Next, we share our ideas with the class.

Did we all solve the problems the same way? What ideas can you try?

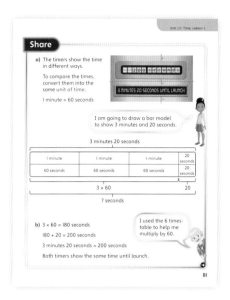

Think together

Then we have a go at some more problems together. Use what you have just learnt to help you.

We will try a challenge too!

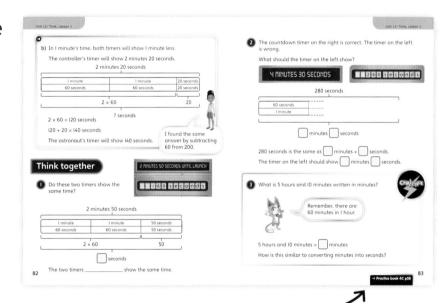

This tells you which page to go to in your **Practice Book**.

At the end of each unit there's an **End of unit check**. This is our chance to show how much we have learnt.

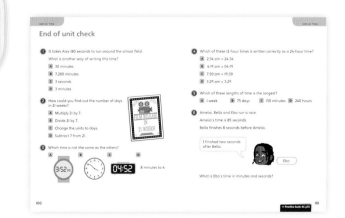

Unit 11
Decimals ❷

In this unit we will ...

⚡ Work out what we need to make a whole

⚡ Write a decimal and represent it on a place value grid

⚡ Compare and order decimals

⚡ Round decimals to the nearest whole number

⚡ Learn the decimal equivalents of fractions such as $\frac{1}{2}$, $\frac{1}{4}$ and $\frac{3}{4}$

⚡ Convert different units of measurement

In the last unit, we learnt how to show a decimal.

What decimal is shown here?

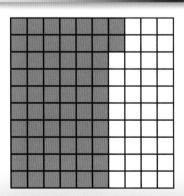

We will need some maths words.
How many of these can you remember?

tenths   hundredths   decimal point

0·1 and 0·01   equivalent   whole number

rounding   greater than (>)

less than (<)   equal to (=)   order

compare   convert   decimal place

ascending   descending

We will also need to know where to find
a decimal on a number line. This will
help us round the number.

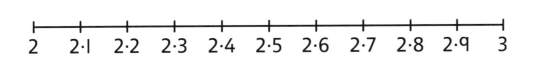

Making a whole

Discover

1   Jamie and Alex both want to make strawberry jam.

   a) How many more kilograms of strawberries does Jamie need to pick?

   b) How many more kilograms of strawberries does Alex need to pick?

8

Share

a) I whole kilogram of strawberries is needed to make the jam.

The number 0·7 is made up of 7 tenths.

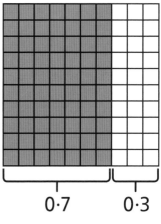

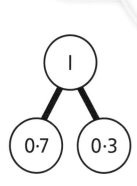

I used a diagram to help me. I know what $\frac{7}{10}$ looks like.

0·7   0·3

3 more tenths are needed to make I whole.

3 tenths = 0·3

Jamie needs to pick another 0·3 kilograms of strawberries.

b) The number 0·46 is made up of 46 hundredths.

Another 54 hundredths are needed to make I whole.

54 hundredths = 0·54

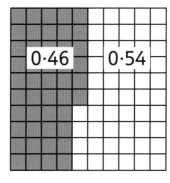

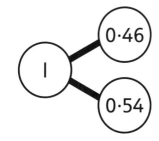

I did not count each one-hundredth needed to make a whole. I noticed that 46 and 54 are a number bond to 100.

Alex needs to pick another 0·54 kilograms of strawberries.

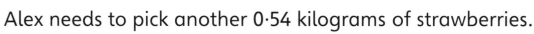

9

Think together

1 Use the models to complete the calculations.

a) 0·☐ + 0·☐ = 1

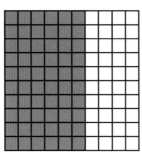 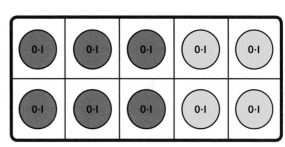

b) 0·☐ + 0·☐ = 1

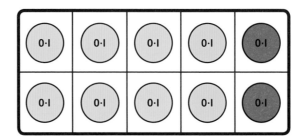

c) 0·☐☐ + 0·☐☐ = 1

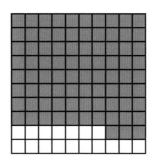

2 Work out the missing numbers in the part-whole models.

a)

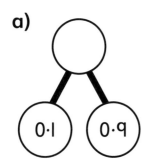

b)

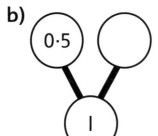

c)

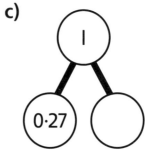

d)

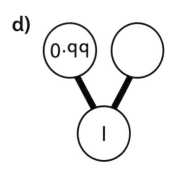

3 Jamilla, Luis and Andy want to fill a jug with 1 litre of water.

a) Jamilla has three cups with different amounts of water in each.

If she pours the water into the jug, how much more water will she need to fill the jug?

b) Luis has three cups with different amounts of water in each.

If he pours the water into the jug, how much more water will Luis need to fill the jug?

> I used a hundredths grid with different colours to represent the cups to help me.

c) Andy has already poured the water from his cups into his jug.

His jug is now full with 1 litre of water.

How much water could have been in each of his cups?

> I wonder if I can find more than 1 answer.

11

Writing decimals

Discover

Make the number 2·37.

Mr Jones

Lexi

1 **a)** What mistake has Lexi made?

b) Show 13·5 on a place value grid.

Share

a) The number 2·37 is made up of:

2 ones   3 tenths   7 hundredths

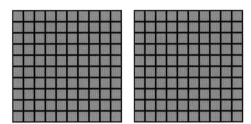   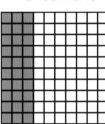   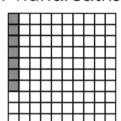

> I know what each digit in a decimal means! The first digit after the decimal point tells me how many tenths. The second digit tells me how many hundredths.

T	O	•	Tth	Hth
	① ①	•	ⓞ·¹ ⓞ·¹ ⓞ·¹	0·01 0·01 0·01 0·01 0·01 0·01
	2	•	3	

2·37 = 2 + 0·3 + 0·07

Lexi's answer shows 2 ones and 3 tenths so this is correct.

Lexi's hundredths column only has 6 hundredths. 2·37 has 7 hundredths, so this is Lexi's mistake.

b) 13·5 has 1 ten, 3 ones and 5 tenths, so 13·5 = 10 + 3 + 0·5.

T	O	•	Tth	Hth
⑩	① ① ①	•	ⓞ·¹ ⓞ·¹ ⓞ·¹ ⓞ·¹ ⓞ·¹	

> There are no hundredths in this number. We do not write the 0 on the end of 13·5.

Think together

1 Work out the missing numbers in the sentences.

T	O	•	Tth	Hth
	① ① ① ① ①	•	⓪·¹ ⓪·¹ ⓪·¹ ⓪·¹	⓪·⁰¹ ⓪·⁰¹ ⓪·⁰¹ ⓪·⁰¹ ⓪·⁰¹ ⓪·⁰¹ ⓪·⁰¹ ⓪·⁰¹ ⓪·⁰¹

a) 5·49 is equal to ⬜ ones, ⬜ tenths and ⬜ hundredths.

$5·49 = 5 + 0·\boxed{} + 0·0\boxed{}$

b) Make the number 0·26 on a place value grid.

O	•	Tth	Hth
	•		

0·26 is equal to ⬜ ones ⬜ tenths and ⬜ hundredths.

$0·26 = \boxed{} + \boxed{}$

2 Match each place value grid to the correct decimal.

a)

O	•	Tth	Hth
	•		⓪·⁰¹ ⓪·⁰¹ ⓪·⁰¹

b)

O	•	Tth	Hth
	•	⓪·¹ ⓪·¹ ⓪·¹	

c)

O	•	Tth	Hth
	•	⓪·¹ ⓪·¹ ⓪·¹	⓪·⁰¹ ⓪·⁰¹ ⓪·⁰¹

| 3·3 | 0·3 | 0·03 | 0·33 | 33 |

3 Ebo has used five counters to make the number 20·12.

10s	1s	•	$\frac{1}{10}$ s	$\frac{1}{100}$ s
●●		● •	●	●●

How many different numbers can you make using the same grid and five counters?

10s	1s	•	$\frac{1}{10}$ s	$\frac{1}{100}$ s
		•		

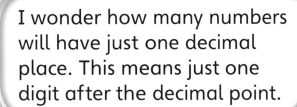

I remember from earlier that $\frac{1}{10}$ is the same as 0·1 and $\frac{1}{100}$ is the same as 0·01.

I wonder how many numbers will have just one decimal place. This means just one digit after the decimal point.

CHALLENGE

15

Comparing decimals

Discover

I think my sunflower is the tallest.

No, mine is the tallest!

0·67 m

0·76 m

Bella

Zac

1 **a)** Who is correct, Bella or Zac? Work out whether to use a < or > sign in the box.

0·67 m ◯ 0·76 m

b) Another sunflower is 0·79 metres tall. Zac thinks this sunflower is taller than his sunflower.

Is Zac correct? How do you know?

16

Share

I put the numbers in a place value grid. To compare the numbers, I started by looking at the tenths.

a) The numbers 0·67 and 0·76 both have 0 ones.

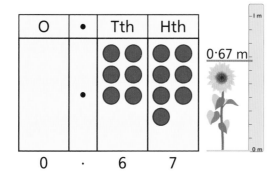

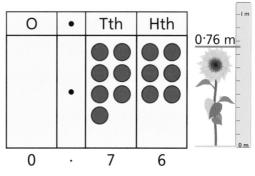

O	•	Tth	Hth
0	·	6	7

O	•	Tth	Hth
0	·	7	6

0·67 has 6 tenths and 0·76 has 7 tenths.

So, 0·76 is the largest number.
Zac is correct.

0·67 m < 0·76 m

I did not need to look at the hundredths column to compare the numbers.

> < means less than or fewer than
> > means greater than

b) Zac's sunflower is 0·76 metres tall.

0·76 = 7 tenths + 6 hundredths
0·79 = 7 tenths + 9 hundredths

0·79 has more hundredths than 0·76.
So, 0·79 is greater than 0·76.
Zac is correct.

0·76 and 0·79 have the same number of tenths.

To compare the numbers, I think I should look at the hundredths.

Think together

1 Holly and Jen are competing in the long jump.

Holly's jump was 2·4 metres. Jen's jump was 2·7 metres.

Who jumped the farthest?

Holly 2·4 m

O	•	Tth
	•	

Jen 2·7 m

O	•	Tth
	•	

2·4 = ☐ ones and ☐ tenths

2·7 = ☐ ones and ☐ tenths

☐ is greater than ☐

☐ > ☐

_____ jumped the farthest.

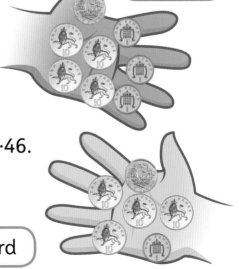

Max

Richard

2 **a)** Max has £1·43. Richard has £1·41.

Who has the most money?

b) Richard finds another 5p. He now has £1·46.

Who has the most money now?

Aki has some pairs of numbers.

	3 tens + 4 tenths + 2 hundredths	or

T	O	•	Tth	Hth
3	I	•	I	2

 or **3·24**

a) Which is the greatest number in each pair?

b) Which is the greatest number overall?

I am going to put each number on a place value grid and start by looking at the I0s.

I will try writing each number out as a decimal first. Then I will compare them by looking at the place value columns from the left.

→ Practice book 4C p12

Ordering decimals

Discover

1 **a)** Order the rabbits from the lightest to the heaviest.

 b) A fourth rabbit, Flopsy, is weighed.

 Flopsy is the second heaviest out of the four rabbits.

 What might Flopsy's mass be?

Share

I will put the numbers into a place value grid. To order the numbers, I need to start by looking at the largest place value.

a)

Molly

O	•	Tth	Hth
●●	•	●	●●●●●
2	•	1	5

Lily

O	•	Tth	Hth
●	•	●●	●●●●●
1	•	2	5

Bob

O	•	Tth	Hth
●●	•	●	●
2	•	1	1

1·25 has 1 one and the others have 2 ones, so Lily is the lightest rabbit.

Molly

O	•	Tth	Hth
●●	•	●	●●●●●
2	•	1	5

Bob

O	•	Tth	Hth
●●	•	●	●
2	•	1	1

Next, I will compare the tenths. Both 2·15 and 2·11 have 1 tenth.

So next I need to compare the hundredths.

2·15 has 5 hundredths.
2·11 has 1 hundredth.
So 2·15 is the largest number.
Molly weighs the most.

Lily is the lightest, Bob is second lightest and Molly is the heaviest.

Lightest ⟶ Heaviest

Lily
1·25 kg

Bob
2·11 kg

Molly
2·15 kg

b) Flopsy's mass is between Bob's and Molly's, so between 2·11 kilograms and 2·15 kilograms.

Her mass must have hundredths that are bigger than 1 but smaller than 5. Flopsy's mass could be 2·12 kilograms, 2·13 kilograms or 2·14 kilograms.

Think together

1 Order the numbers from smallest to largest.

2·1		
O	•	Tth

1·2		
O	•	Tth

1·9		
O	•	Tth

Smallest ⬚ , ⬚ , ⬚ Largest

2 Put the numbers in order from largest to smallest.

15·62   25·31   19·07

T	O	•	Tth	Hth
1	5	•	6	2
2	5	•	3	1
1	9	•	0	7

Largest ⬚ , ⬚ , ⬚ Smallest

The numbers have all been placed in the same place value grid.

Does this help?

3 Write these numbers on a place value grid from smallest to largest.

1·43   2·33   1·53

O	•	Tth	Hth
	•		

Smallest

↓

Largest

4 **a)** The numbers below are ordered from largest to smallest.

One of the numbers is in the wrong place.

9·46,   9·34,   9·82,   9·28,   9·08

Which number is in the wrong place?

b) Put a digit in each box so the numbers are in ascending order.

5·3☐,   5·☐3,   ☐·54,   6·☐9,   6·1☐

CHALLENGE

I wonder if there is more than one answer.

Ascending means from smallest to largest.

23

→ Practice book 4C p15

Rounding decimals

Discover

① a) Round the amount of sugar to the nearest whole number.

Is Mo correct?

b) What is the smallest possible amount of salt to one decimal place?

Share

a) There are 6·8 grams of sugar in the cereal.

6·8 is between 6 and 7 so I drew a number line going up in tenths to help me round the number.

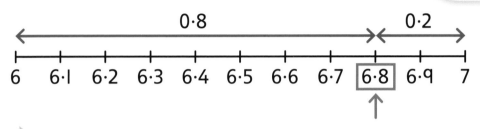

Look at the tenths. If there are 5 or more tenths, then we round up to the next whole number.

8 tenths is '5 or more', so 6·8 rounded to the nearest whole number is 7.

Mo is correct. The amount of sugar is closer to 7 grams than 6 grams.

b)

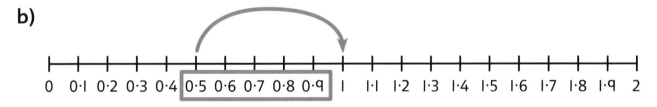

To find the smallest possible amount of salt, you need to look at the numbers below 1.

To round to the nearest whole number, you need to look at the tenths which are 5 or more.

The smallest possible amount of salt is 0·5 grams.

I know 1 is between 0 and 2.

I drew a different number line to help me decide.

Think together

1 **a)** Work out the missing numbers in the sentences.

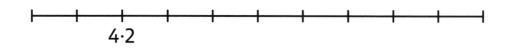

4·2

4·2 is between ⬜ and ⬜ .

4·2 rounded to the nearest

whole number is ⬜ .

> Look at the tenths. If there are 4 or fewer tenths, then we round down to the last whole number.

b) 12·5 is between ⬜ and ⬜ .

12·5 rounded to the nearest whole number is ⬜ .

2 Jamilla says if she rounds all these numbers to the nearest whole number, they all round to 8.

Is Jamilla correct? Explain your answer.

7·5, 8·5, 8·1, 7·7, 7·9

> I looked at the number of tenths to help me round.

7   8   9

3 **a)** Max rounds 70·8 to the nearest whole number.

Lexi rounds Max's answer to the nearest 10.

Kate rounds Lexi's answer to the nearest 100.

What answers did Max, Lexi and Kate get?

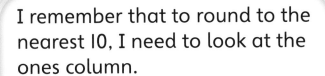

> I remember that to round to the nearest 10, I need to look at the ones column.
>
> To round to the nearest 100, I need to look at the tens column.

b) Max starts with a different number and rounds to the nearest whole number.

Lexi rounds Max's answer to the nearest 10.

Kate rounds Lexi's answer to the nearest 100 again and gets 500.

What number could Max have started with?

> I wonder if drawing more number lines could help with this question.

→ Practice book 4C p18

Halves and quarters

Discover

There are 0·5 litres of orange juice in this jug. 0·5 is the same as $\frac{1}{2}$.

Ebo

There are 0·7l litres of orange juice in this jug. 0·7l is the same as $\frac{3}{4}$.

Amelia

This jug is $\frac{1}{2}$ full.

This jug is $\frac{3}{4}$ full.

1 **a)** Is Ebo correct that 0·5 is equivalent to $\frac{1}{2}$? Explain your answer.

b) Amelia is incorrect. What is $\frac{3}{4}$ as a decimal?

Share

a) Ebo's jug is $\frac{1}{2}$ full.

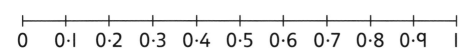

> I remember where $\frac{1}{2}$ is on a number line. I know that $\frac{1}{2}$ means 1 out of 2 equal parts.

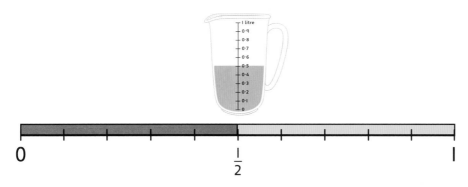

We can see that $\frac{1}{2}$ is equivalent to 0·5, so Ebo is correct.

b) Amelia's jug is $\frac{3}{4}$ full.

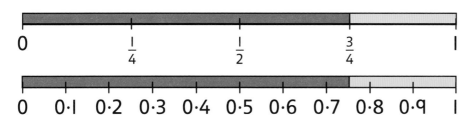

$\frac{3}{4}$ is exactly half-way between 0·7 and 0·8.

So, $\frac{3}{4}$ is equivalent to 0·75.

> I did it a different way. I can see that $\frac{3}{4}$ of the 100 squares are coloured. That is 75 squares. Each square is equal to 1 hundredth.

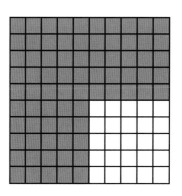

75 hundredths = 0·75

So $\frac{3}{4}$ as a decimal is 0·75.

Think together

1 Write $\frac{1}{4}$ as a decimal.

$\frac{1}{4}$ is equivalent to ☐ hundredths.

$\frac{1}{4}$ = 0·☐☐

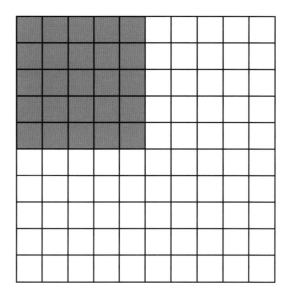

2 Discuss with a partner how you could use the diagram to show $\frac{1}{2}$ as a decimal.

$\frac{1}{2}$ is equivalent to ☐ hundredths.

$\frac{1}{2}$ is equivalent to ☐ tenths.

$\frac{1}{2}$ = 0·☐

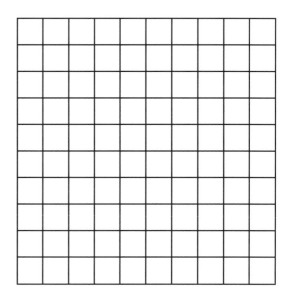

3 a) One of these diagrams is not equivalent to the rest.

Which diagram shows the odd one out? How do you know?

CHALLENGE

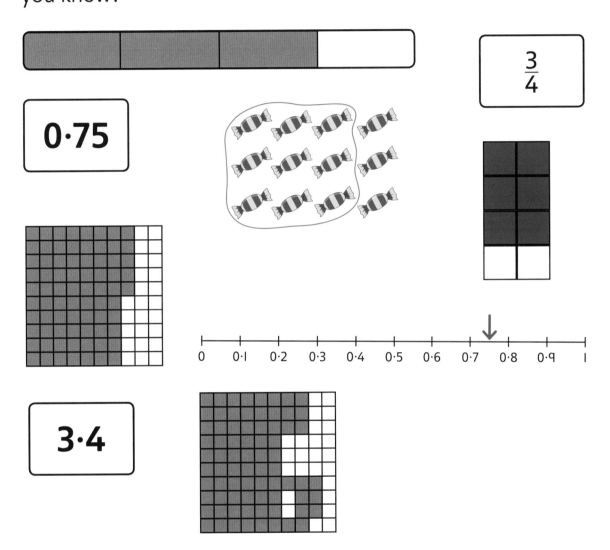

b) Show how many different ways you can represent the number 0·25.

I think it would help to write a decimal or a fraction for each diagram. Then I could use my knowledge of equivalent fractions and decimals.

31

→ Practice book 4C p21

Problem solving – decimals

Discover

I a) What is the mass of I cube?

b) What is the mass of the cylinder?

Share

a)

300 g	
?	?

I drew a bar model to help me find the solution. To work out the mass of 1 cube, I need to divide 300 by 2.

The mass of 2 cubes is 300 grams.

$300 \div 2 = 150$ g. The mass of 1 cube is 150 grams.

b) The total mass of the 10 cubes is

$150 \times 10 = 1{,}500$ g.

The masses are in different units. I need to make them the same to work out the mass of the cylinder.

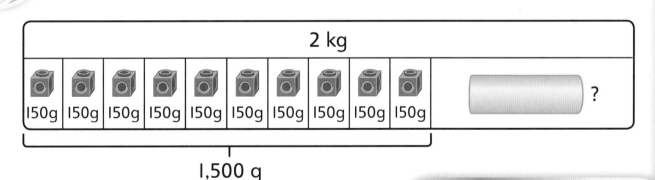

2 kg

| 150g | 150g | 150g | 150g | 150g | 150g | 150g | 150g | 150g | 150g | | ? |

1,500 g

1,000 grams = 1 kilogram. To change kilograms to grams, multiply by 1,000.

2 kg $= 2 \times 1{,}000$ g $= 2{,}000$ g

$2{,}000 - 1{,}500 = 500$ g.

The mass of the cylinder is 500 grams.

Think together

1 Use the conversions to help you find the solutions.

a) 7 kilograms = ☐ grams

b) 3,600 g = ☐ kg and ☐ g

1 km	1,000 m

1 kilometre = 1,000 metres

c) 9 kilometres = ☐ metres

d) 7,300 m = ☐ km and ☐ m

1 litre = 1,000 millilitres

e) 6,000 millilitres = ☐ litres

f) 5 l and 300 ml = ☐ ml

2 Luis wants to swim 1 kilometre.

1 pool length = 50 metres

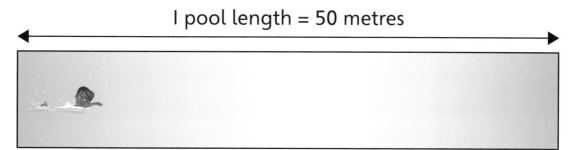

How many lengths does Luis need to swim?

I think I know how many metres are in 1 kilometre. Now I just need to work out how many lengths of 50 metres fit into this.

3 **a)** How many centimetres are there in 1 metre?

CHALLENGE

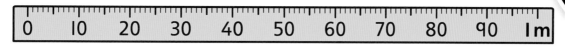

0   10   20   30   40   50   60   70   80   90   1 m

There are ☐ centimetres in 1 metre.

b) Use your answer to part a) to convert these amounts.

i)   700 cm = ☐ m

ii) 12 m = ☐ cm

iii) 450 cm = ☐ m and ☐ cm

iv) ☐ cm = 3 m and 95 cm

→ Practice book 4C p24

End of unit check

1 Which number completes the calculation?

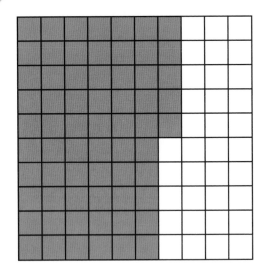

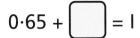 0·65 + ☐ = 1

A 1·65   B 0·66   C 0·45   D 0·35

2 2 ones, 5 tenths and 3 hundredths is equal to:

A 253   B 352   C 2·53   D 25·3

3 These numbers are listed in order from the smallest to the largest. What could the digit missing from the box be?

3·46   3·79   4·28   4·2☐   4·38

A 7   B 0   C 9   D 3

4 Which of the following numbers does not round to 6 when rounded to the nearest whole number?

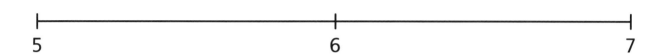

5   6   7

A 6·5   **B** 6·2   **C** 5·5   **D** 5·9

5 Which of the following is equal to 7,060 grams?

A 70 kg and 60 g

B 7 kg and 600 g

C 7 kg and 60 g

D 7 kg and 6 g

6 How many kilograms does the bag of sugar weigh? Explain your thinking.

Unit 12
Money

In this unit we will …

⚡ Write money in pounds and pence, using a decimal point

⚡ Order, add and subtract amounts of money

⚡ Round money to the nearest 10p or nearest £1

⚡ Find change

⚡ Solve simple word problems involving money

Do you know how to work out how much money there is? Remember to add the pounds first and then the pence.

We will need some maths words.
Do you know what they all mean?

notes   coins   pounds (£)   pence (p)

add   subtract   change

round to the nearest   order

greater than (>)   less than (<)

cheaper   more expensive   estimate

over estimate   under estimate

total   notation

We need to be able to add and subtract using column methods.

56p + 89p

56p + 89p = 145p

145p = £1 and 45p

```
  H  T  O
     5  6
+    8  9
  1  4  5
     1  1
```

Pounds and pence

Discover

1 **a)** How much money does Bella have in pence?

b) How much money does Bella have in pounds and pence?

Key 1p 2p 5p 10p 20p 50p £1 £2

Share

I circled coins which made 100p.

a) 50p + 50p = 100p

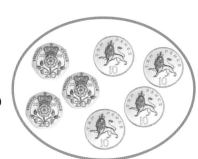

20p + 20p + 20p + 10p + 10p + 10p + 10p = 100p

10p + 10p + 5p + 5p + 2p + 2p + 1p + 1p = 36p

100p + 100p + 36p = 236p

Bella has 236p.

Remember, 100p is equal to £1.

b) There is 200 pence, so that makes 2 pounds.

There is 36 pence left over.

That makes £2 and 36p.

Bella has £2·36.

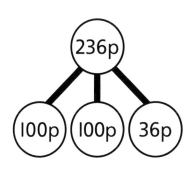

We use a decimal point to separate the whole pounds from the pence.

Think together

1 Lexi is counting her money.

a) How much money does Lexi have in pence?

Lexi has ☐ pence.

b) How much money does Lexi have in pounds and pence?

Lexi has ☐ pounds and ☐ pence.

c) Show this using the pound sign and a decimal point.

£ ☐ . ☐ ☐

We are writing the amount in pounds and do not use a p.

2 How much money is in the purse?

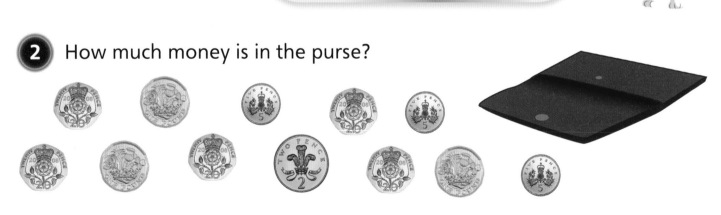

There is £ ☐ . ☐ ☐ in the purse.

42

Key 1p 2p 5p 10p  20p 50p £1 £2

3 Emma and Danny are comparing how much money they have.

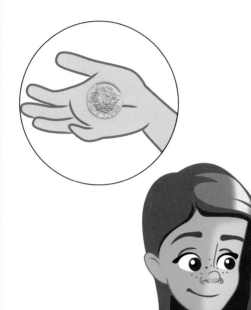

I have more money than you because I have ten coins and you only have one.

Emma

Danny

Do you agree with Danny?

Explain why.

I wonder how many 10p pieces make a pound. This will help me work out how much Emma has.

 £5 £10 £20 £50

43

→ Practice book 4C p29

Pounds, tenths and hundredths

Discover

I **a)** How much money does Emma have?

How much money does Danny have?

b) How much money shows heads for Emma?
Give the answer in pounds.

How much money shows heads for Danny?
Give the answer in pounds.

Key 1p 2p 5p 10p 20p 50p £1 £2

Share

a) Emma has 100 1p coins.

100 × 1p = 100p

100 pence is equal to £1.

Emma has £1.

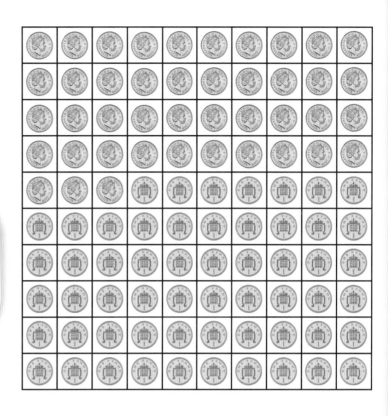

> 1p is $\frac{1}{100}$ of £1. If the £1 is the whole, then 1p is a hundredth of the whole.

Danny has 10 10p coins.

10 × 10p = 100p

100 pence is equal to £1.

Danny also has £1.

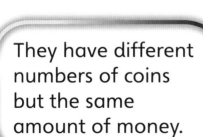

> 10p is $\frac{1}{10}$ of £1. If the £1 is the whole, then 10p is a tenth of the whole.

> They have different numbers of coins but the same amount of money.

 £5　 £10　 £20　 £50

b) There are 43 1p coins showing heads.

This is $\frac{43}{100}$.

$\frac{43}{100} = 0\cdot43$

Emma has £0·43 showing heads.

There are 7 10p coins showing heads. This is $\frac{7}{10}$.

Danny has £0·70 showing heads.

Remember, the decimal point separates the pounds from the pence.

We do not write Danny's money as £0·7.

Seven 10p coins are equal to 70 pence. So we write it as £0·70 (0 pounds and 70 pence).

Think together

1 How much money in pounds is shown on each grid?

a)

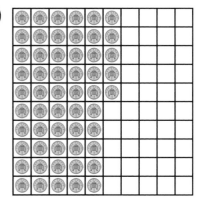

There are ☐ 1p coins.

This is equal to ☐ .

There is £ ☐ · ☐ ☐ .

b)

There are ☐ 10p coins.

This is equal to ☐ .

There is £ ☐ · ☐ ☐ .

46

Key 1p 2p 5p 10p 20p 50p ☐£1 ☐£2

2 How much money in pounds is there in each box?

A

C

B
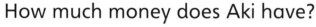

D

There is £ ☐·☐☐ in box A.   There is £ ☐·☐☐ in box C.

There is £ ☐·☐☐ in box B.   There is £ ☐·☐☐ in box D.

3 **a)** Aki has three-tenths of £1.

How much money does Aki have?

b) Lexi has $\frac{17}{100}$ of £1.

How much money does Lexi have?

c) Mo has £1. He loses $\frac{9}{100}$ of £1.

How much money does Mo have left?

I remember that 10p is $\frac{1}{10}$ of £1 and 1p is $\frac{1}{100}$ of £1.

 £5   £10   £20   £50

→ Practice book 4C p32

Ordering amounts of money

Discover

Isla

1 **a)** Put the items in order from least to most expensive.

b) Which items could Isla buy with the money she has?

Key 1p 2p 5p 10p 20p 50p £1 £2

Share

a) Convert the amounts to pence.

> To order the items, I converted them to the same notation and then put them on a number line.

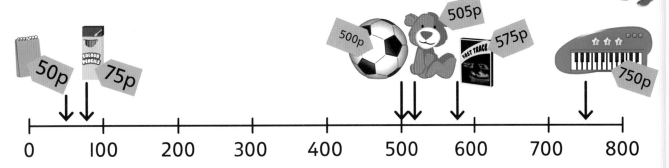

50p 75p 500p 505p 575p 750p

| | | | | | | | | |
|0|100|200|300|400|500|600|700|800|

The items in order from least to most expensive are: notepad, pack of pencils, football, teddy bear, computer game and musical keyboard.

b) Isla has a £5 note.

Isla could buy any items that cost 5 pounds or 500 pence or less.

So she could buy the football, because that is exactly £5, or she could buy the pencils and notepad.

75p < 500p   £0·50 < £5

She could not buy the teddy bear as it costs more than 500p.

505p > 500p

 £5   £10   £20  £50

Think together

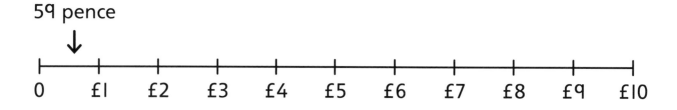

a) Which is the cheapest item on the shelf?

The cheapest item on the shelf is _____ .

b) Which is the most expensive item on the shelf?

The most expensive item on the shelf is _____ .

c) Order the items from the least to the most expensive.

d) Now order the items from the most expensive to the least expensive.

2 Alex has these coins.

Which of the toys could Alex buy?

Alex could buy _____ .

Key 1p 2p 5p 10p 20p 50p £1 £2

3

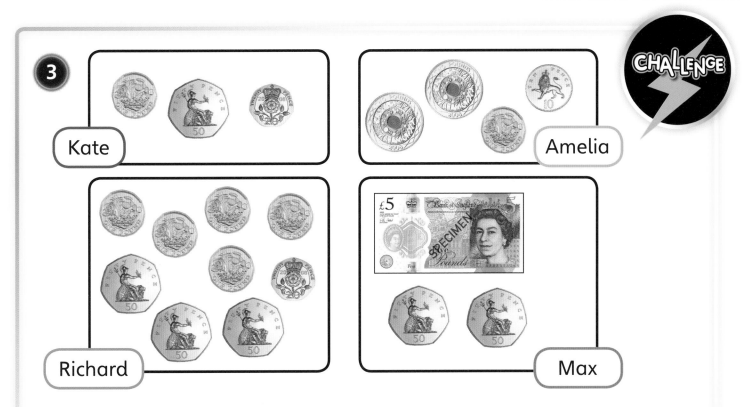

Kate

Amelia

CHALLENGE

Richard

Max

Kate, Amelia, Richard and Max are comparing how much money they have.

Max

I have the most money as I have a £5 note.

No, I have the most money as I have the greatest number of coins.

Richard

I will put the numbers in order and see if either of them are correct.

I think one of them might be right, but it is not for the right reason.

What mistakes have Max and Richard made?

 £5   £10   £20    £50

→ Practice book 4C p35

Rounding money

Discover

1 a) Round each number to the nearest 10p.

b) Round each number to the nearest pound.

Why might Ebo and Zac be rounding their numbers?

Key 1p 2p 5p 10p 20p 50p £1 £2

Share

a) 27p lies between 20p and 30p.

I notice that the difference between 27 and 20 is 7 and the difference between 27 and 30 is 3.

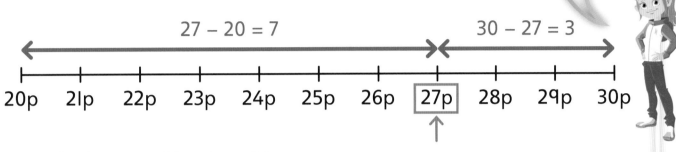

27 − 20 = 7   30 − 27 = 3

20p 21p 22p 23p 24p 25p 26p 27p 28p 29p 30p

27p is closer to 30p than 20p.

So 27p rounded to the nearest 10p is 30p.

£4·32 lies between £4·30 and £4·40.

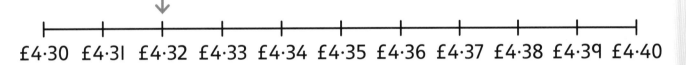

£4·30 £4·31 £4·32 £4·33 £4·34 £4·35 £4·36 £4·37 £4·38 £4·39 £4·40

£4·32 rounded to the nearest 10p is £4·30.

£5·95 lies between £5·90 and £6·00.

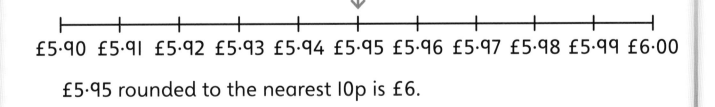

£5·90 £5·91 £5·92 £5·93 £5·94 £5·95 £5·96 £5·97 £5·98 £5·99 £6·00

£5·95 rounded to the nearest 10p is £6.

What about £5·95? It is in the middle. I think I round up to £6·00.

Maths has a rule: when a number is in the middle, we round up.

 £5   £10   £20   £50

53

b)

27p rounds to £0 to the nearest pound.

£4·32 rounds to £4 to the nearest pound.

£5·95 rounds to £6 to the nearest pound.

Ebo and Zac might be rounding a number to the nearest 10p or pound to work out a quick estimate of the total cost or to estimate the difference between two amounts.

Think together

1) **a)** Round £1·68 to the nearest 10 pence.

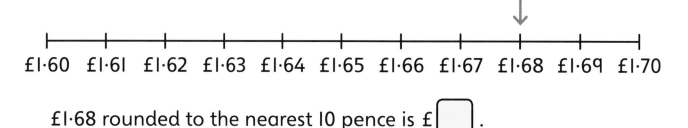

£1·68 rounded to the nearest 10 pence is £⬜.

b) Round £1·68 to the nearest pound.

£1·68 rounded to the nearest pound is £⬜.

Key 1p 2p 5p 10p 20p 50p £1 £2

2 **a)** Round £3·25 to the nearest ten pence.

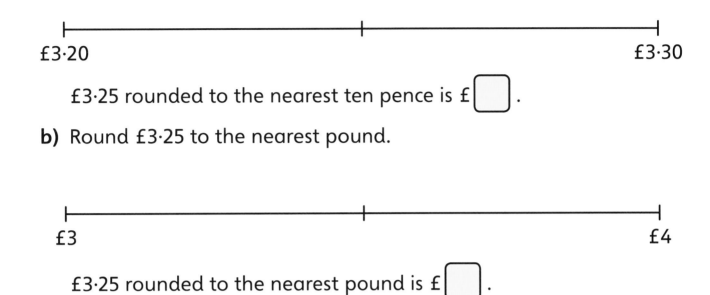

£3·20   £3·30

£3·25 rounded to the nearest ten pence is £ ☐ .

b) Round £3·25 to the nearest pound.

£3   £4

£3·25 rounded to the nearest pound is £ ☐ .

3 Which of the following round to £3 when rounded to both the nearest 10p **and** nearest pound?

£3·49   £3·04   £3·14

£2·87   £2·25   £2·99

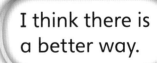

I will work out which numbers round to £3 to the nearest £1 first. Then I will check which ones round to £3 to the nearest 10p.

I think there is a better way.

 £5   £10   £20   £50

55

→ Practice book 4C p38

Using rounding to estimate money

Discover

Let's try to work out an estimate for the total cost of what we need.

I have rounded the price of the eggs. They cost about £1·70.

Bread £1·45

Cereal £3·98

Chocolate £2·10

Oranges £1·19

Milk 89p

Toshi

Jen

1 **a)** Round each item in the trolley to the nearest pound to estimate the total cost.

b) What do you think Jen has rounded the price of the eggs to the nearest?

What is the most the eggs could cost? What is the least they could cost?

Key 1p 2p 5p 10p 20p 50p £1 £2

Share

a)

> I made a table to write my results. The rounded numbers are in the last column. I then added these up.

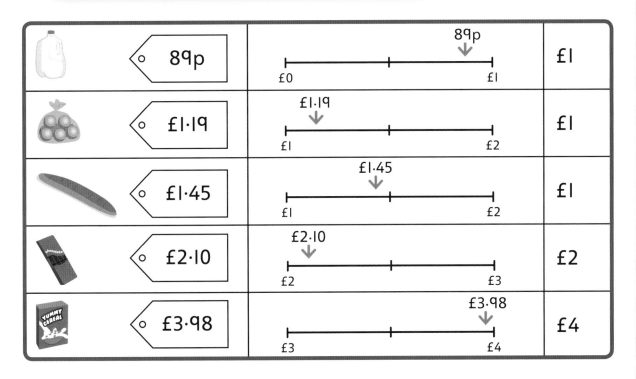

£1 + £1 + £1 + £2 + £4 = £9

An estimate of the total cost is £9.

b) The most the eggs could cost is £1·74.

The least the eggs could cost is £1·65.

> I think Jen has rounded to the nearest 10p. I drew a number line and highlighted the section that would round to £1·70.

£1·60   £1·65   £1·70   £1·74   £1·80

Think together

1 Estimate how much more a box of cereal costs than a loaf of bread.

£1·45 rounds to £ ☐ to the nearest 10p.

£3·98 rounds to £ ☐ to the nearest 10p.

Bread £1·45

Cereal £3·98

YUMMY CEREAL

```
├──┼──┼──┼──┼──┼──┼──┼──┼──┼──┤
0     1     2     3     4     5
```

The cereal costs about £ ☐ more than the loaf of bread.

2 Here are some more items Toshi and Jen want to buy.

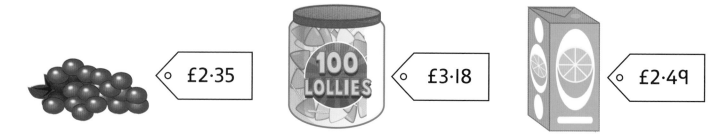

£2·35   100 LOLLIES   £3·18   £2·49

a) Round each item to the nearest £1 to estimate the total cost.

b) Is your answer a good estimate?

Explain your answer to your partner.

c) Do you think your answer is an over estimate or under estimate?

Why?

An **over estimate** is where you think it is more than the actual total. An **under estimate** is where it is less than the actual total.

Key 1p 2p 5p 10p 20p 50p £1 £2

3 Look at the receipt.

Receipt

Butter	£4·75
Potatoes	£1·89
Crisps	£0·87

Find an estimate of the total by:

a) Rounding each item to the nearest £1.

b) Rounding each item to the nearest 10p.

Which estimate was quicker?

Which do you think is more accurate?

I wonder if rounding to the nearest £1 can ever be as accurate as rounding to the nearest 10p.

I remembered to add the pounds and pence separately when I added the costs.

 £5 £10 £20 £50

→ Practice book 4C p41

Problem solving – pounds and pence

Discover

Alex   Holly   Jamie

1 **a)** Alex buys a book, a CD and a t-shirt.

Work out how much Alex spends by thinking about the different coins she could have used.

b) Alex pays for her items with a £10 note.

Work out how much change Alex gets.

60

Key 1p 2p 5p 10p 20p 50p £1 £2

Share

a) These are the coins Alex could have used to buy the different items.

I used a number line to add up the coins.

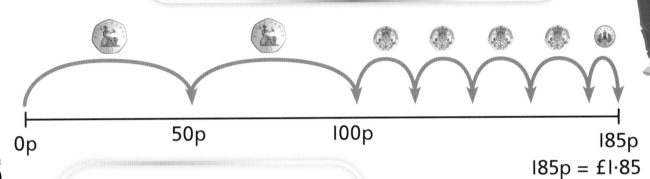

0p   50p   100p   185p

185p = £1·85

I worked it out in a different way. I used a bar model and column addition.

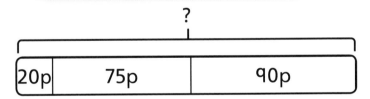

```
  H  T  O
     9  0
     7  5
+    2  0
  ─────────
  1  8  5
     1
```

185p = £1·85

Alex spends £1·85 in total.

b)

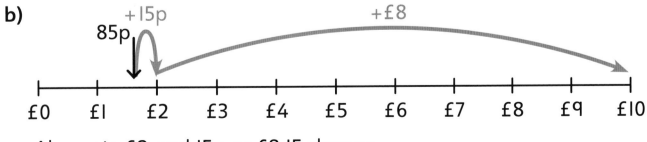

Alex gets £8 and 15p or £8·15 change.

 £5   £10   £20    £50

Think together

1 **a)** What is the total cost of these items?

£1·60   £3·35

£1·60 = £ [ ] and [ ]p   £3·35 = £ [ ] and [ ]p

Add up the pounds.   £[ ] + £[ ] = £[ ]

Add up the pence.   [ ]p + [ ]p = [ ]p

£[ ] and [ ]p = £[ ]

The total cost is £[ ].

b) Work out the total cost of these items.

 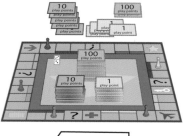

£2·40   £1·75

£2·40 = £ [ ] and [ ]p   £1·75 = £ [ ] and [ ]p

Add up the pounds.   £[ ] + £[ ] = £[ ]

Add up the pence.   [ ]p + [ ]p = [ ]p = £[ ] and [ ]p

The total cost is £[ ].

Key 1p 2p 5p 10p 20p 50p £1 £2

2 Zac spends £2·35. He pays with a £10 note.

How much change will he receive?

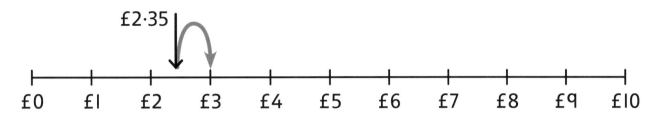

£2·35

£0   £1   £2   £3   £4   £5   £6   £7   £8   £9   £10

Zac will receive £ ⬚ change.

3

CHALLENGE

Ambika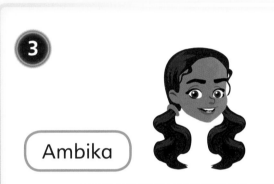

 Bella

Ambika spends £2·68.
She pays with a £5 note.
How much change does
Ambika receive?

Bella buys some items.
She pays with a £5 note.
She gets £3·46 change.
How much does she spend?

What is the same and what is different about the two questions?

I think the
methods are
similar, but the
question is not
the same.

I am going to draw a
bar model to help me
work out the answer to
each question.

 £5 £10 £20 £50

→ **Practice book 4C p44**

Problem solving – multiplication and division

Discover

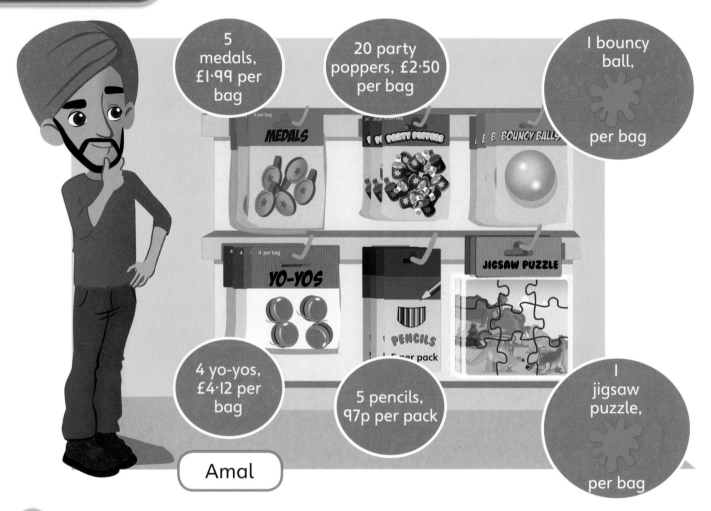

1 **a)** Amal needs 57 party poppers.

How many bags of party poppers does he need to buy?

How much does it cost Amal to buy the bags?

b) The cost of three bouncy balls is £1·26.

How much does one bouncy ball cost?

Key 1p 2p 5p 10p 20p 50p £1 £2

Share

a) One bag contains 20 party poppers.

Amal needs 57 party poppers.

I will count up in 20s until I get to 57. I can tell from the number line that Amal cannot buy 57 exactly.

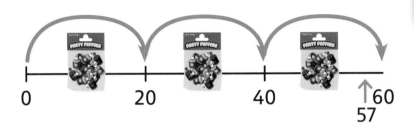

Amal needs to buy 3 bags of party poppers.
Each bags costs £2·50.

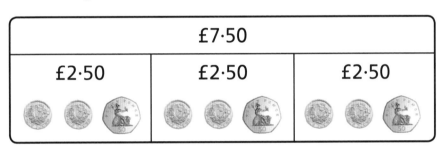

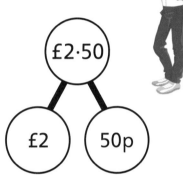

£2 × 3 = £6   50p × 3 = £1·50

£6 + £1·50 = £7·50

The total cost of 3 bags of party poppers is £7·50.

b) £1·26 = 126 pence

I changed the price to pence and then used a part-whole model to help me divide.

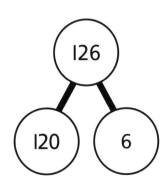

120 ÷ 3 = 40

6 ÷ 3 = 2

So, 126 ÷ 3 = 42p.

One bouncy ball costs 42p.

 £5   £10   £20   £50

Think together

1 Amal is buying some more items.

a) How much do 6 bags of yo-yos cost?

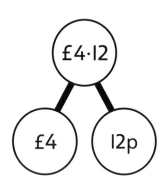

4 per bag

YO-YOS

£4·12 per bag

$6 × £4 = \boxed{}$ $6 × 12p = \boxed{}$

$£\boxed{}$ and $\boxed{}p = £\boxed{}$

6 bags of yo-yos cost $£\boxed{}$.

b) How much do 4 packs of pencils cost?

```
    9  7
 ×     4
 _____

 _____
```

97p per pack

PENCILS

5 per pack

$4 × 97p = \boxed{}p$

$\boxed{}p = £\boxed{}$

4 packs of pencils cost $£\boxed{}$.

Key 1p 2p 5p 10p 20p 50p £1 £2

2 Jen buys 5 jigsaw puzzles.

The total cost is £4·55.

How much does each jigsaw puzzle cost?

£4·55 = ☐ p

☐ p ÷ 5 = ☐ p

Each jigsaw puzzle costs ☐ p.

3 Sofia goes shopping. Here is part of her receipt.

Receipt

4 tins of beans	£1·48
2 bread rolls	£0·84
5 packets of rice	£6·30

a) How do you know a packet of rice costs more than £1 without doing the division?

b) How much does one of each item cost?

I split 148p into 120p and 28p.

I wonder why you did not use 140 and 8.

Solving two-step problems

Discover

That is £2·50.

Why not try to work out the total cost in your head?

5 × 26p ...

Holly

26p each

24p each

28p each

p each

p each

p each

Toshi

Luis

1 Luis wants to buy 5 apples and 5 oranges.

  a) Luis has started to work out the total cost. Complete his method.

  b) How do you think Holly worked out the total cost so quickly?

68 **Key** 1p 2p 5p 10p 20p 50p £1 £2

Share

a) Multiply to work out the cost of 5 apples.

I worked out of the cost of the apples and oranges and then added them.

$5 \times 20p = 100p$

$5 \times 6p = 30p$

$5 \times 26 = 130p$

130p = £1·30

26p	26p	26p	26p	26p

Now work out the cost of 5 oranges.

120p = £1·20

24p	24p	24p	24p	24p

Add the cost of the apples and oranges.

To multiply 26 by 5, I first multiplied by 10 and then divided by 2.

$130p + 120p = 250p = £2·50$

The total cost is £2·50.

b) Holly may have worked out the total cost of 1 apple and 1 orange and then multiplied by 5.

26p + 24p = 50p

5 × 50p = 250p = £2·50

26p	24p	26p	24p	26p	24p	26p	24p	26p	24p

Think together

26p each

1 The cost of 1 apple and 2 bananas is 94p.

Work out the cost of 1 banana.

94p

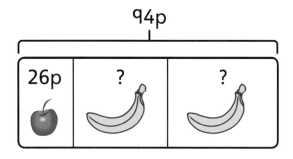

| 26p | ? | ? |

94p − 26p = ☐

☐ ÷ 2 = ☐

A banana costs ☐ p.

2 A pineapple and 2 mangoes costs £1 and 83p.

A pineapple and 1 mango costs £1 and 51p.

How much does a pineapple cost?

£1 and 83p   £1 and 51p

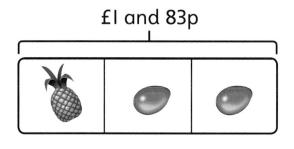   

A pineapple costs £ ☐ and ☐ p.

Key 1p 2p 5p 10p 20p 50p £1  £2

3

CHALLENGE

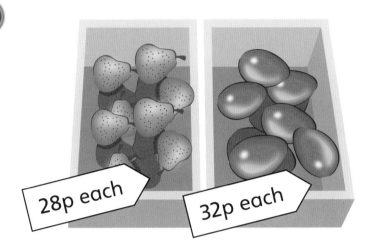

28p each

32p each

Luis works out the total cost of 6 mangoes and 4 pears.

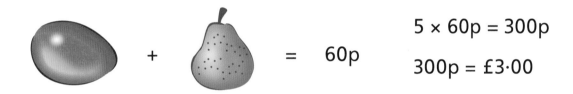

= 60p

5 × 60p = 300p

300p = £3·00

a) Explain the mistake Luis has made.

b) Work out the correct answer.

Explain your method.

I do not think I can do the same as I did earlier.

I think I can use the same method as there are still 10 items.

Problem solving – money

Discover

1 a) Kate wants to buy 3 buns at the cheapest price.

Should she buy a pack of buns for £1·50 or 3 single buns for 65p each?

b) Max buys one pack of 6 buns for £3·50.

Is this the best deal?

Key 1p 2p 5p 10p 20p 50p £1 £2

Share

a) An individual bun costs 65p.

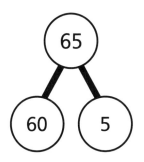

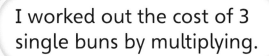

I worked out the cost of 3 single buns by multiplying.

$3 \times 60p = 180p$

$3 \times 5p = 15p$

I worked out the cost of 1 bun by dividing 150p by 3. This was 50p per bun, which is cheaper than 65p.

$180p + 15p = 195p = £1·95$

A bag of 3 buns costs £1·50.

£1·95 > £1·50 so it is cheaper for Kate to buy the pack of 3 buns.

b) Max could buy 6 single buns instead of a 6-pack of buns.

$6 \times 60p = 360p$

$6 \times 5p = 30p$

$6 \times 65p = 390p$

390p = £3·90					
65p	65p	65p	65p	65p	65p

Or Max could buy 2 packs of 3 buns.

£3	

The cost of 2 packs of 3 buns is £3. This is cheaper than £3·50.

Max could have got a better deal.

Think together

1. Kate has three goes on the hook-a-duck stall.

   How much change does she get from £5?

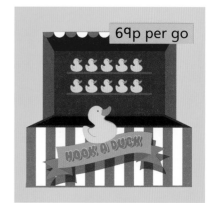

69p per go

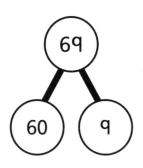

$3 \times 60p = \boxed{}p$

$3 \times 9p = \boxed{}p$

$3 \times 69p = \boxed{}p$

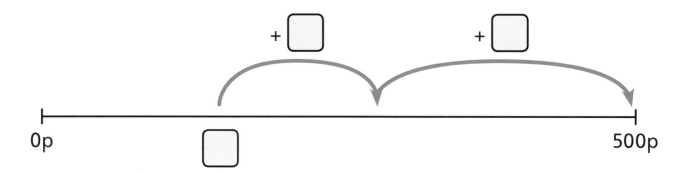

$+ \boxed{}$ $+ \boxed{}$

0p $\boxed{}$ 500p

Kate receives £ $\boxed{}$. $\boxed{}$ $\boxed{}$ change from £5.

2. Bella buys 10 raffle tickets.

   She gets £6·60 change from £10.

   a) How much did Bella spend on raffle tickets?

   b) How much does each raffle ticket cost?

Key 1p 2p 5p 10p 20p 50p £1 £2

3

Deal 1:
bag of 4 cookies
for £2·40

Deal 2:
bag of 6 cookies
for £3·36

I think the bag of 4
cookies is the best deal.

Lee

Is Lee correct?

Explain your method.

I worked out the cost of
1 cookie from each bag.

I worked out the cost of
12 cookies from each bag.

 £5 £10 £20 £50

→ Practice book 4C p53

End of unit check

1 How much money is shown here?

| A | £10 | B | £71 | C | £3·67 | D | £4·67 |

2 What is this amount in pounds?

| A | £3 | B | £0·30 | C | £0·3 | D | £0·03 |

3 Which item is the most expensive?

A £12·50

B £9·73

C 950p

D £12 and 43 pence

Key 1p 2p 5p 10p 20p 50p £1 £2

4 Adam buys a cup of tea with a £5 note.

He receives £3·15 change.

How much did the cup of tea cost?

A £1·85   **B** £2·15   **C** £2·85   **D** £3·15

5 Which of the following amounts does not round to £8 to the nearest £1?

A £7·50   **B** £7·90   **C** £8·04   **D** £8·50

6 What do you get if you add together £1·34 and 72p?

A £1·96   **B** £2·06   **C** £73·34   **D** You cannot add them together.

7 A pencil costs 17p.

Max buys 9 pencils for his friends.

He pays with a £5 note.

How much change does Max get?

8 How much does an apple cost?

 + + + = 95p

 + + = 75p

 £5   £10   £20   £50

→ **Practice book 4C p56**

Unit 13
Time

In this unit we will ...

⚡ Convert between units of time
⚡ Write times in different ways
⚡ Compare times by converting units
⚡ Solve problems about units of time

How many minutes are in one hour?

5 minutes

Here are some maths words we will be using. Are any of these words new?

convert	compare	units of time
seconds	minutes	hours
days	weeks	months
years	12-hour	24-hour
analogue	digital	am/pm

Which time do you think is shortest? Why?

600 seconds

9 minutes

$\frac{1}{4}$ of an hour

Units of time ❶

Discover

❶ **a)** Do the two countdown timers show the same time until launch?

b) What will both timers say in 1 minute's time?

Share

a) The timers show the time in different ways.

To compare the times, convert them into the same **unit of time**.

1 minute = 60 seconds

I am going to draw a bar model to show 3 minutes and 20 seconds.

3 minutes 20 seconds

1 minute	1 minute	1 minute	20 seconds
60 seconds	60 seconds	60 seconds	20 seconds

3 × 60   20

200 seconds

3 × 60 = 180 seconds

180 + 20 = 200 seconds

3 minutes 20 seconds = 200 seconds

Both timers show the same time until launch.

I used the 6 times-table to help me multiply by 60.

b) In I minute's time, both timers will show I minute less.

The controller's timer will show 2 minutes 20 seconds.

2 minutes 20 seconds

I minute	I minute	20 seconds
60 seconds	60 seconds	20 seconds

2 × 60   20

? seconds

$2 \times 60 = 120$ seconds

$120 + 20 = 140$ seconds

The astronaut's timer will show I40 seconds.

I found the same answer by subtracting 60 from 200.

Think together

2 MINUTES 50 SECONDS UNTIL LAUNCH

II60 seconds

I Do these two timers show the same time?

2 minutes 50 seconds

I minute	I minute	50 seconds
60 seconds	60 seconds	50 seconds

2 × 60   50

☐ seconds

The two timers _____ show the same time.

2 The countdown timer on the right is correct. The timer on the left is wrong.

What should the timer on the left show?

┌────────────────────────────────┐
│   **4 MINUTES 30 SECONDS**   │
└────────────────────────────────┘

┌────────────────────────────────┐
│   2 8 0   s e c o n d s   │
└────────────────────────────────┘

280 seconds

```
┌──────────────────────────────────────────────┐
│ ┌─────────────────┐ ┌ ─ ─ ─ ┐                │
│ │   60 seconds    │ │       │                │
│ ├─────────────────┤ │       │                │
│ │    I minute     │ │       │                │
│ └─────────────────┘ └ ─ ─ ─ ┘                │
└──────────────────────────────────────────────┘
```

☐ minutes ☐ seconds

280 seconds is the same as ☐ minutes + ☐ seconds.

The timer on the left should show ☐ minutes ☐ seconds.

3 What is 5 hours and 10 minutes written in minutes?

Remember, there are 60 minutes in I hour.

5 hours and 10 minutes = ☐ minutes

How is this similar to converting minutes into seconds?

→ Practice book 4C p58

Units of time ②

Discover

1 a) In how many days will the new play area open?

   b) How old is Max's dog?

Share

a) The new play area will be open in 4 weeks. Convert this into days.

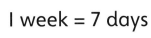

I am going to draw a bar model to work out the number of days in 4 weeks.

4 weeks

I week	I week	I week	I week
7 days	7 days	7 days	7 days

28 days

I week = 7 days

$4 \times 7 = 28$ days

The new play area will open in 28 days.

b) Max's dog is I year 7 months older than 3 years 8 months.

I think I will add the number of whole years first. Then I will add the number of months.

3 years + I year = 4 years

8 months + 7 months = 15 months

15 months	
12 months	3 months

I year   3 months

15 months is the same as I year and 3 months.

4 years + I year and 3 months = 5 years and 3 months

Max's dog is 5 years and 3 months old.

Think together

I am 8 years and 10 months old.

Reena

I am 4 months older than you.

Andy

a) How old is Andy?

8 years 10 months + 4 months = 8 years ☐ months

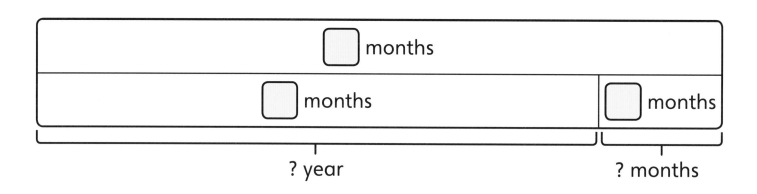

☐ months

☐ months

☐ months

? year

? months

☐ months is the same as ☐ year ☐ months.

8 years + ☐ year ☐ months = ☐ years ☐ months

Andy is ☐ years and ☐ months old.

b) Mo is I year and II months older than Reena.

How old is Mo?

Mo is ☐ years and ☐ months old.

86

2 How many weeks are the same as 35 days?

35 days

7 days

$\boxed{}$ × 7 days = $\boxed{}$ weeks

$35 \div 7 = \boxed{}$

$\boxed{}$ weeks are the same as 35 days.

3 What is 4 years and 3 months converted into months?

I think that 4 years and 3 months is the same as 43 months.

Amelia

I will think about how many months are in a year.

Explain Amelia's mistake.

Work out the correct answer.

→ Practice book 4C p61

Converting times ❶

Discover

❶ a) What should the time on the watch say now?

b) What will the clock and the watch look like when the spies meet back at the bench?

Share

a) **Analogue** and **digital** are two ways of showing times. You can convert from one to the other.

The park clock shows an analogue time.

It shows the time is seven minutes past 3.

5 minutes

2 minutes

The time on the watch should say 3:07 pm.

hour

minutes past

> 'am' times are before midday (starting from midnight); 'pm' times are after midday (up to midnight).

b) An hour and a half is the same as I hour 30 minutes.

3:07 pm   4:07 pm   4:37 pm

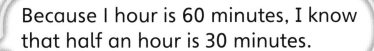

+ I hour   + 30 mintues

> Because I hour is 60 minutes, I know that half an hour is 30 minutes.

analogue   digital

When the spies meet back at the bench, the clock and the watch will look like this:

Think together

1. What will this time look like as an analogue time and as a digital time?

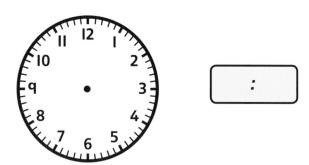

Meet me at the park bench at twenty to nine in the morning.

Twenty to 9 is the same as ☐ minutes past ☐ .

2. Match the analogue and digital clocks.

a)
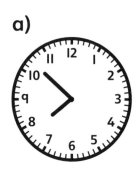

b)
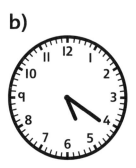

c)

d)

4:05 AM

7:51 PM

5:21 PM

8:10 AM

3 Three children have tried to draw this time on their clock faces.

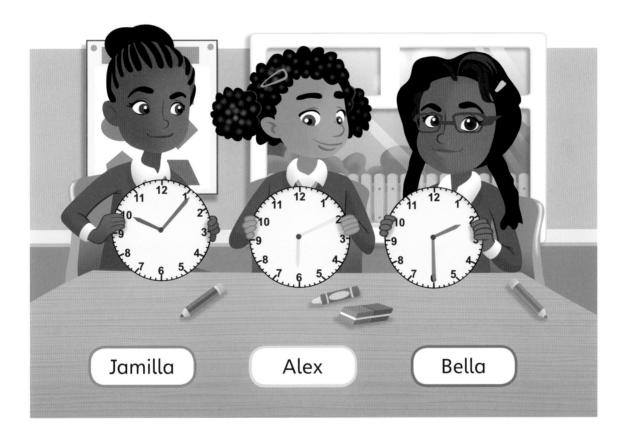

Whose clock face matches the digital time?

What mistakes have the other two children made?

First I will look at the hour hand, then the minute hand.

→ Practice book 4C p64

Converting times ❷

Discover

1. a) Why do the watches show four digits?

   b) The clock is correct. Which watch shows the right time?

Share

a) All the digital watches show 24-hour times.

24-hour digital times are always written using four digits.

The first two digits show the hour (from 00 up to 23).

The last two digits show the number of minutes past (from 00 up to 59).

24-hour times do not include 'am' or 'pm'. We know by looking at the numbers. Times from 00:00 to 11:59 are am times. Times from 12:00 to 23:59 are pm times.

hours	:	minutes past
06	:	30
09	:	17
13	:	45
15	:	52
19	:	00

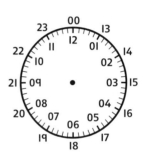

b) The time on the clock is eight minutes to 4. This is the same as fifty-two minutes past 3.

The shop is open, so this is a pm time.

I can convert a 12-hour pm time into a 24-hour time by adding 12 to the number of hours.

3 + 12 = 15

3:52 pm = 15:52

The correct watch looks like this:

15:52

Think together

1 What will these times look like as 24-hour times?

a) The clock shows ☐ minutes past ☐.

As a 12-hour time, this is written as ☐ : ☐ am.

As a 24-hour time, this is written

as ☐ : ☐.

in the
morning

b) The clock shows ☐ minutes to ☐.

As a 12-hour time, this is written as ☐ : ☐ pm.

☐ + 12 = ☐

As a 24-hour time, this is written as ☐ : ☐.

at night

2 Quarter to 5 is the same as ☐ minutes past ☐.

How would you complete the analogue and 24-hour digital clock if this time was in the morning?

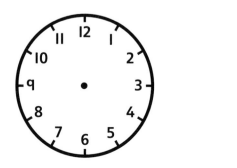

☐ : ☐

3 Mo is altering his digital watch to show 24-hour times.

It is twenty-five to 7.

a) What would Mo's watch now show if this was an am time?

b) What would it show if it was a pm time?

4

I know how to convert this to a 24-hour time! I add 12 to the number of hours to get 19:28.

7:28 AM

Isla

CHALLENGE

Explain Isla's mistake.

How would you convert 7:28 am into a 24-hour time?

I know how many digits a 24-hour time has.

→ Practice book 4C p67

Problem solving – units of time

Discover

1 a) How many years have the explorers been training for this expedition?

b) Does Toshi have enough socks to make it to the North Pole?

Share

> I am going to use a bar model to help convert 30 months into years.

a) The explorers have been training for 30 months.

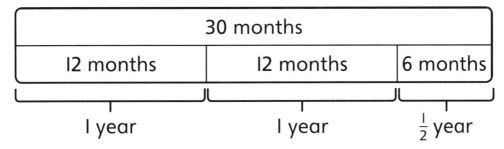

30 months		
12 months	12 months	6 months
1 year	1 year	$\frac{1}{2}$ year

12 months = 1 year

6 months = $\frac{1}{2}$ a year

30 months = 12 months + 12 months + 6 months

The explorers have been training for $2\frac{1}{2}$ years.

b)

> I converted the weeks into days to help compare them.

3 weeks

1 week	1 week	1 week
7 days	7 days	7 days

21 days

$3 \times 7 = 21$

Toshi has enough socks for 21 days.

It takes 20 days to get to the North Pole. 21 days > 20 days.

Toshi does have enough socks to make it to the North Pole!

> I found the same answer by converting the days into weeks instead. 3 weeks > 2 weeks 6 days.

97

Think together

1   Who is quicker at putting their socks on in the cold?

It takes me 3 minutes and 14 seconds to put my socks on in the cold.

Jen

It takes me 203 seconds.

Toshi

3 minutes 14 seconds

1 minute	1 minute	1 minute	14 seconds
☐ seconds	☐ seconds	☐ seconds	14 seconds

☐ seconds

3 minutes 14 seconds

= (3 × 60) + 14

= ☐ + 14

= ☐ seconds

Use >, < or = to compare the times.

☐ seconds ◯ 203 seconds

I can think of a different way to convert these times to find the answer!

 is quicker than _____ .

2 Which tin of food needs to be used first?

Find the answer in two ways.

A   B

a) Convert tin A into weeks and compare the weeks.

Tin A

30 days

7 days	7 days	7 days	7 days	2 days
☐ week	☐ week	☐ week	☐ week	2 days

☐ weeks ☐ days

Tin ____ needs to be used first.

b) Convert tin B into days and compare the days.

Tin ____ needs to be used first.

3 How could you compare:

CHALLENGE

a) 3 hours and 45 minutes to 200 minutes?

b) 4 $\frac{1}{2}$ years to 50 months?

What operations did you use in each part?

To compare measurements, convert one of the measurements so that the units are the same in both.

99

End of unit check

1 It takes Alex 180 seconds to run around the school field.

What is another way of writing this time?

A 30 minutes

B 7,200 minutes

C 3 seconds

D 3 minutes

2 How could you find out the number of days in 21 weeks?

A Multiply 21 by 7.

B Divide 21 by 7.

C Change the units to days.

D Subtract 7 from 21.

3 Which time is not the same as the others?

A   B   C   D

8 minutes to 4

4 Which of these 12-hour times is written correctly as a 24-hour time?

A 2:34 am = 24:34

B 4:19 am = 04:19

C 7:30 am = 19:30

D 3:29 am = 3:29

5 Which of these lengths of time is the longest?

A 1 week   B 75 days   C 150 minutes   D 240 hours

6 Amelia, Bella and Ebo run a race.

Amelia's time is 85 seconds.

Bella finishes 8 seconds before Amelia.

I finished two seconds after Bella.

Ebo

What is Ebo's time in minutes and seconds?

→ Practice book 4C p73

Unit 14
Statistics

In this unit we will ...

⚡ Present data in pictograms, bar charts and tables

⚡ Explore line graphs

⚡ Solve problems based on data

We are going to meet this type of graph in this unit. What was the temperature at 10 am?

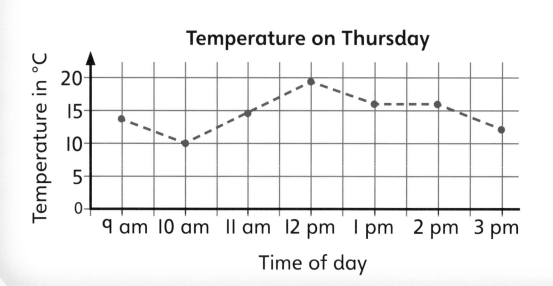

Temperature on Thursday

Temperature in °C / Time of day

We will need some maths words. Which ones have you seen before?

data　　　　line graph　　　　pictogram

bar chart　　　table　　　altogether

more than　　　greatest　　　smallest

continuous data　　　compare

We need this too! How many people's favourite colour is yellow?

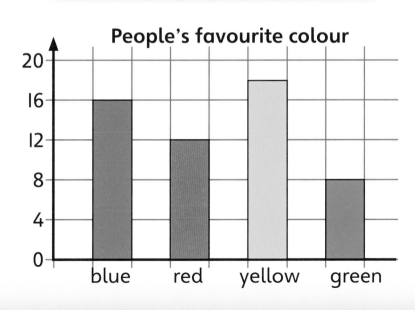

People's favourite colour

Charts and tables ❶

Discover

Number of items baked in Class 4T

	Number
cupcakes	⬭⬭⬭⬭⬭
gingerbread men	⬭⬭⬭⬭
cookies	⬭⬭⬭⬭◖

Each ⬭ represents 10 items.

Number of items baked in Class 4A

❶ a) How many cookies did each class make?

b) Which item did Class 4A make the most of? How many did they make?

Share

a) Each ◯ in the **pictogram** represents 10 items.

Each ◖ represents 5 items.

The row for cookies has 4 and a half ◯.

◯ ◯ ◯ ◯ ◖

10 + 10 + 10 + 10 + 5 = 45

Class 4T made 45 cookies.

> I did it another way. I multiplied 4 × 10 then added 5.

> I am going to use a ruler to make sure I am reading the correct values.

Number of items baked in Class 4A

In the **bar chart**, the bar for cookies lines up half-way between 50 and 60 on the vertical axis.

Class 4A made 55 cookies.

b) The highest bar in the bar chart is for cupcakes.

Class 4A made more cupcakes than any other item.

The top of the cupcake bar lines up with 60 on the vertical axis.

Class 4A made 60 cupcakes.

Number of items baked in Class 4A

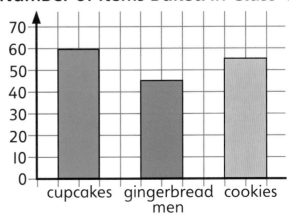

Think together

Number of items sold in Class 5T

	Number
cupcakes	◯ ◯ ◯ ◖
gingerbread men	◯ ◯ ◯ ◸
cookies	◯ ◯ ◯ ◯ ◯

Each ◯ represents 8 items.

Number of items sold in Class 5A

1 **a)** How many cupcakes did each class sell?

Each ◯ represents ⬚ .

Each ◖ represents ⬚ .

◯   ◯   ◯   ◖

⬚ + ⬚ + ⬚ + ⬚ = ⬚

Class 5T sold ⬚ cupcakes.

The bar for cupcakes is half-way between ⬚ and ⬚ .

Class 5A sold ⬚ cupcakes.

b) How many gingerbread men did Class 5T sell?

Class 5T sold ⬚ gingerbread men.

I think ◸ must represent a quarter of a ◯.

2 The table shows how many cupcakes and gingerbread men two more classes sold.

	Class 4B	Class 4C
cupcakes	8	15
gingerbread men	12	6

Cupcakes were sold for £2. Gingerbread men were sold for £1.

Which class raised the most money?

3 Some children are raising money for charity. The bar chart shows the amount each year group raised.

a) How much did Year 3 raise?

b) Year 6 raised £675.

The bar should be half-way between £600 and £700.

Olivia

Is Olivia correct?

Explain your answer.

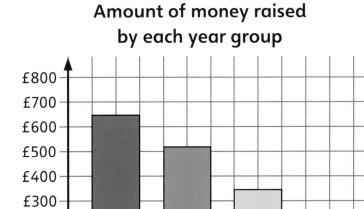

Amount of money raised by each year group

c) How much did the year groups raise altogether?

107

→ Practice book 4C p75

Charts and tables ②

Discover

Number of tickets sold on Saturday

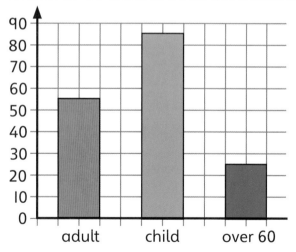

Number of tickets sold on Sunday

	Number
adult	▭ ▭ ▭ ▭ ◖
child	▭ ▭ ▭ ▭ ▭ ◖
over 60	▭ ▭ ◖

Each ▭ represents 12 tickets.

1 **a)** How many more child tickets did the farm sell on Saturday?

b) How many adult (under 60) tickets did the farm sell altogether over the weekend?

Share

a) The bar for child tickets is half-way between 80 and 90. 85 child tickets were sold on Saturday.

Each ⬜ represents 12 people.
Each ◖ represents 6 people.

5 × 12 = 60
60 + 6 = 66

The farm sold 66 child tickets on Sunday.

85 − 66 = 19

The farm sold 19 more child tickets on Saturday.

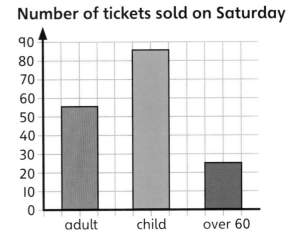

Number of tickets sold on Saturday

> I did this another way. I added
> 12 + 12 + 12 + 12 + 12 + 6 to get the answer.

b) The farm sold 55 adult tickets on Saturday.

There are four and a half symbols for adult tickets on the pictogram.

4 × 12 = 48
48 + 6 = 54

The farm sold 54 adult tickets on Sunday.

55 + 54 = 109

The farm sold 109 adult tickets altogether over the weekend.

> I need to add a value from the bar chart to a value on the pictogram.

Think together

Number of children feeding baby animals

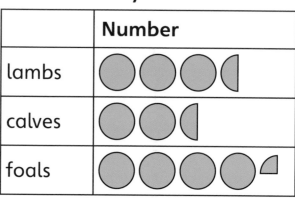

Each ⬤ represents 12 children.

1 **a)** How many more children than adults fed the lambs?

Each ⬤ represents ☐ children.

Each ◖ represents ☐ children.

☐ × ☐ = ☐

☐ + ☐ = ☐

The lambs bar for adults is half-way between ☐ and ☐ .

☐ adults fed the lambs.

☐ – ☐ = ☐

☐ more children than adults fed the lambs.

Number of adults feeding baby animals

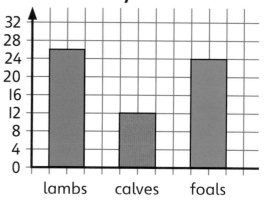

b) How many people fed the foals altogether?

☐ children fed the foals.

☐ adults fed the foals.

☐ + ☐ = ☐

☐ people fed the foals altogether.

2 The pictograms show the amount of money made at a café on Saturday and Sunday.

Money made from meals sold on Saturday

	Number
adult hot	◯◯◖
adult cold	◯◗
child hot	◯◯◢
child cold	◯◯◯

Each ◯ represents £100.

Money made from meals sold on Sunday

	Number
adult hot	◯◯◢
adult cold	◯◖
child hot	◯◯◯◗
child cold	◯◯◢

Each ◯ represents £100.

a) How much money did the café make from hot meals on Sunday?

b) How much more money did the café make from cold children's meals on Saturday compared to Sunday?

3 The bar chart shows the opinion of visitors to the farm on Saturday and Sunday.

CHALLENGE

a) How many more visitors rated the farm ok on Saturday than Sunday?

b) Did more people rate the farm on Saturday or Sunday?

■ represents Saturday.
☐ represents Sunday.

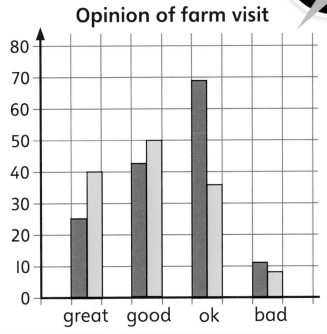

Opinion of farm visit

great   good   ok   bad

III

Line graphs ❶

Discover

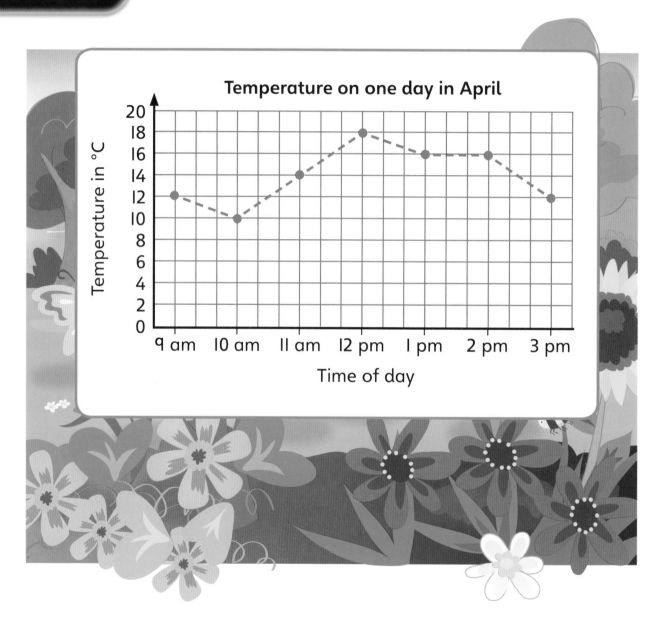

① **a)** What is the temperature at 11 am?

b) How much does the temperature decrease by between 12:30 pm and 3 pm?

Share

a) Find 11 am on the horizontal axis of the **line graph**.

Then move up to the line.

Read along to see which temperature this corresponds to.

The temperature at 11 am is 14 °C.

I am going to use a ruler to help me.

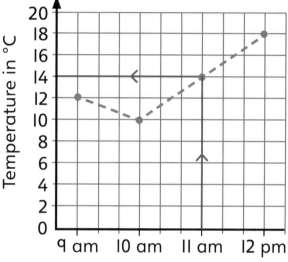

b) The temperature at 12:30 pm is 17 °C.

The temperature at 3 pm is 12 °C.

17 − 12 = 5

The temperature decreases by 5 °C between 12:30 pm and 3 pm.

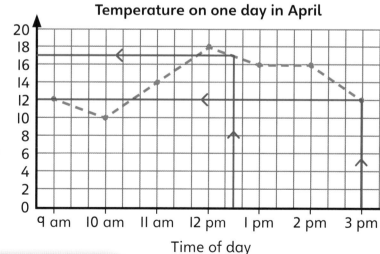

Temperature on one day in April

I read off the values from 12:30 pm and 3 pm and found the difference.

113

Think together

This line graph shows the temperature inside Emily's house on Tuesday.

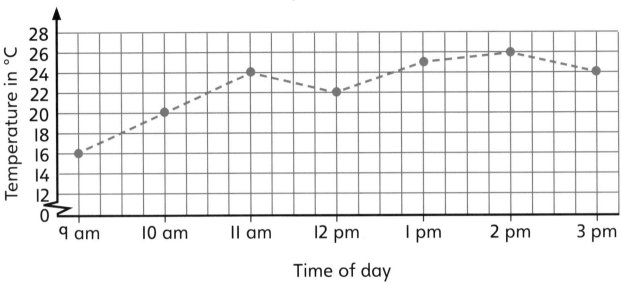

Temperature inside

Temperature in °C

Time of day

1 **a)** What was the temperature at 11 am?

b) What was the temperature at 1 pm?

c) What was the temperature at 2:30 pm?

d) At what time was it the warmest inside Emily's house?

e) At what time was the temperature 21 °C?

2 For how long is the temperature above 24 °C in Emily's house?

I am going to start by going across from the temperature on the vertical axis.

3 The temperature in a small town was measured on the first day of October and the first of December.

The results are shown on the line graph below.

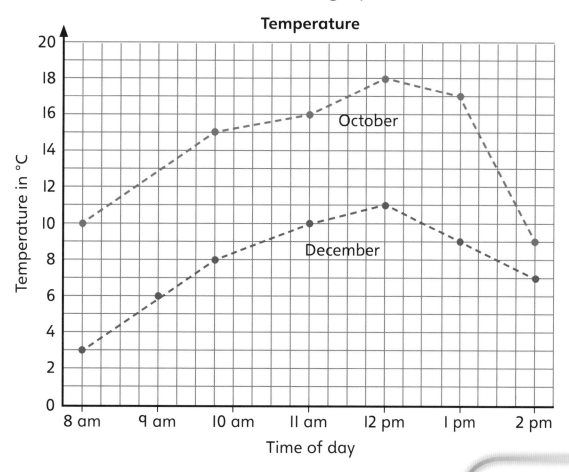

a) What was the temperature at midday on 1 December?

b) What is the difference in the temperature at 2 pm on 1 December and 2 pm on 1 October?

c) What is the same and what is different about the temperature on 1 October and 1 December?

Line graphs can show more than one set of data. Each set of data has its own line.

115

Line graphs ②

Discover

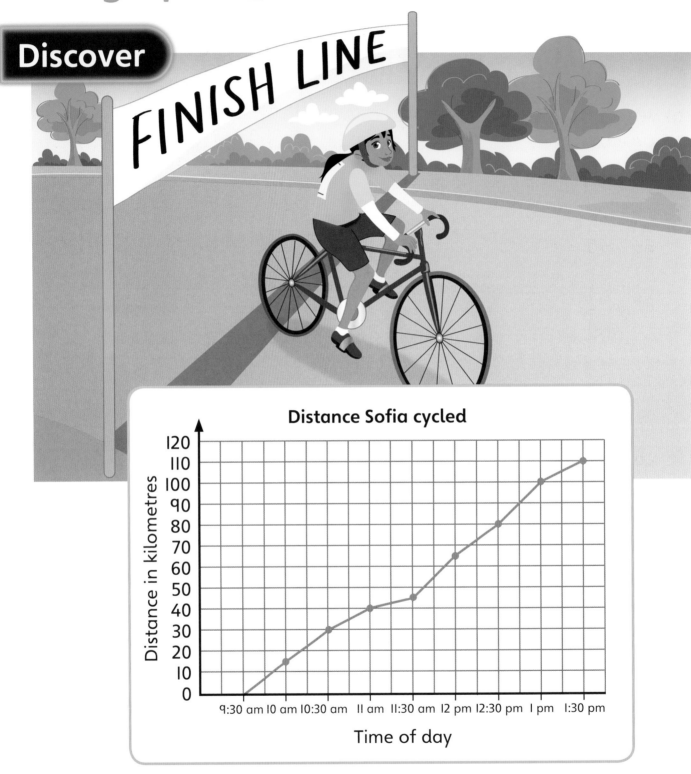

Distance Sofia cycled

1 a) How far did Sofia cycle between 11 am and 12 pm?

b) How long did it take Sofia to travel the next 40 km after 12 pm?

Share

I am going to work out the distance Sofia had travelled at 11 am and at 12 pm and then find the difference.

a) At 11 am Sofia had cycled 40 km.

At 12 pm Sofia had cycled 65 km.

$65 - 40 = 25$

Sofia cycled 25 km between 11 am and 12 pm.

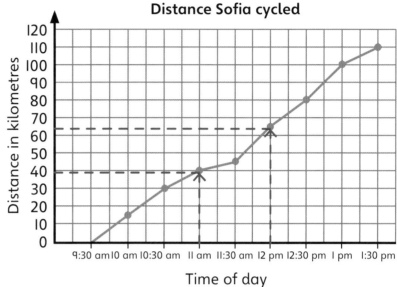

Distance Sofia cycled

b) Sofia had cycled 65 km by 12 pm.

$65 + 40 = 105$ km

Sofia had travelled 105 km by 1:15 pm.

It took Sofia 1 hour and 15 minutes to travel the next 40 km.

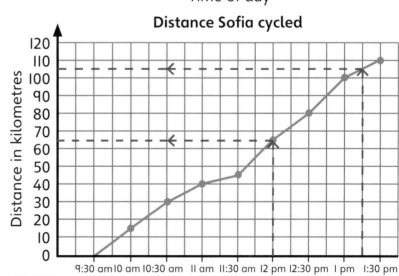

Distance Sofia cycled

The data is **continuous** so at any point on the graph it shows how far Sofia has cycled.

I need to start by looking for the distances on the vertical axis.

Think together

Toshi takes part in a cycle race. The graph shows Toshi's journey.

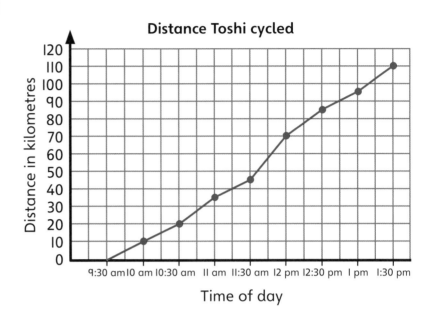

Distance Toshi cycled

1. **a)** How far did Toshi travel between 12:30 pm and 1:30 pm?

Toshi had travelled ☐ km by 12:30 pm.

Toshi had travelled ☐ km by 1:30 pm

☐ − ☐ = ☐

Toshi travelled ☐ km between 12:30 pm and 1:30 pm.

b) How far did Toshi travel between 11:15 am and 12:45 pm?

c) What time do you think the race started?

d) Do you think it is the same race that Sofia took part in?

2. How long did it take Toshi to travel from 20 km to 70 km?

Toshi had travelled 20 km at ☐ .

Toshi had travelled 70 km at ☐ .

Toshi took ☐ hours to travel between 20 km to 70 km.

3 This graph shows the progress of two athletes in a running race.

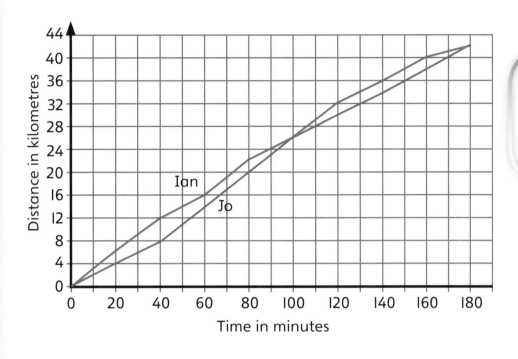

I am going to be careful and look at the correct line for each person.

a) Complete these sentences.

After 60 minutes Ian had run ☐ km and Jo had run ☐ km.

It took Jo ☐ minutes and Ian ☐ minutes to run 34 km.

Before the end of a race, Ian and Jo had both run exactly the

same distance after ☐ minutes.

The length of the running race was ☐ km.

b) Write five more things that you can tell from the graph.

Use some of the words below to help you.

most, compared to, least, fastest, slowest, further, more, less

119

→ Practice book 4C p84

Problem solving – graphs

Discover

1 a) How much more money did Years 3 and 4 raise in total compared to Years 5 and 6?

b) Year 4 raised money by selling cards for £2 each.

How many cards did they sell in total?

Share

I need to work out how much Years 3 and 4 raised altogether first.

a) Year 3 raised £110.

Year 4 raised £120.

£120 + £110 = £230

Years 3 and 4 raised £230 altogether.

Year 5 raised £130.

Year 6 raised £70.

£130 + £70 = £200

Years 5 and 6 raised £200 altogether.

£230 − £200 = £30

Years 3 and 4 raised £30 more than Years 5 and 6.

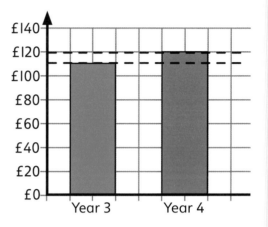

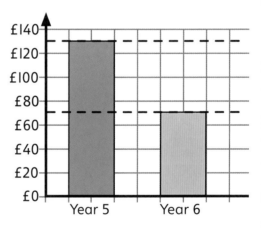

b) Year 4 raised £120.

£120 ÷ £2 = 60

Year 4 sold 60 cards in total.

I can work out how many cards Year 4 sold by using division.

Think together

1. This graph shows how much money was raised by each class.

   How much more money did Maple and Ash classes raise in total compared to Oak and Willow classes in total?

   Amount of money raised by class

   ⬚ + ⬚ = ⬚

   ⬚ + ⬚ = ⬚

   ⬚ − ⬚ = ⬚

   Maple and Ash classes raised £⬚ more than Oak and Willow classes.

   a) How much money did the four classes raise altogether?

   The classes raised £⬚ altogether.

   b) Each child in Oak class raised £5. How many children are in Oak class?

   £⬚ ÷ £⬚ = ⬚

   There are ⬚ children in Oak class.

I can use some of my working from part a) to help me work out part b).

2 The pictogram shows the number of soft toys Year 3 sold at a summer fair.

a) Which soft toys did Year 3 sell more than 10 of?

b) Each soft toy sold for £5.

How much money did selling lions and dogs make?

Lions and dogs made £ ☐ for Year 3.

Type of soft toy sold by Year 3

	Number
lions	●●●●●●●
dogs	●●●
cats	●◖
owls	●●●●●◖

Each ● represents 2 soft toys.

3 Year 5 raised money by selling CDs of a class concert. Oak class sold 7 CDs. Each class sold CDs for the same amount.

Use the clues below to complete the table and work out how much money they raised in total.

Maple	£ ☐
Ash	£ ☐
Oak	£42
Willow	£ ☐

I am going to work out how much Oak charged for each CD first.

Willow collected £12 less than Oak.

Maple collected $\frac{8}{10}$ of the amount Willow collected.

Ash collected $\frac{1}{2}$ more than Maple's total amount.

123

End of unit check

1 How many more people prefer a cat than prefer a rabbit?

A $1\frac{3}{4}$

B 7

C 9

D 10

Favourite pet

	Number
cat	●●●●◁
dog	●●●
rabbit	●●◖
hamster	●●●◖

Each ● represents 4 people.

2 Which statement is not true?

A The most popular pet is a cat.

B The least popular pet is a rabbit.

C 4 more people like hamsters than like rabbits.

D 3 people's favourite pet is a dog.

3 This table shows the scores out of 100 of 4 children in their termly spelling tests.

Which child showed the biggest improvement between Autumn term and Summer term?

A Otis

B Grace

C Evie

D Milo

	Autumn term	Summer term
Otis	73	93
Grace	21	71
Evie	42	93
Milo	32	81

How I travel to school

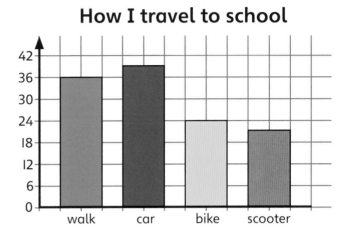

4 Sam asked some children in Year 4 how they came to school today.

He put his results in a bar chart.

How many people came by scooter?

A 20

C 21

B 24

D $18\frac{1}{2}$

5 How many more people walked, biked or scootered to school in total compared to the number of people who came by car?

A 6

B 3

C 40

D 42

6 What is the difference between the highest and lowest temperature in the day?

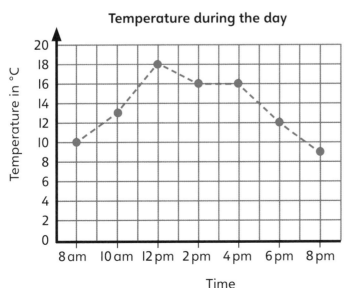

Temperature during the day

125

→ Practice book 4C p90

Unit 15
Geometry – angles and 2D shapes

In this unit we will ...
- ⚡ Learn to recognise obtuse, acute and right angles
- ⚡ Understand regular and irregular shapes
- ⚡ Name and describe quadrilaterals and triangles
- ⚡ Identify lines of symmetry in shapes and patterns

Do you remember quarter turns and half turns?

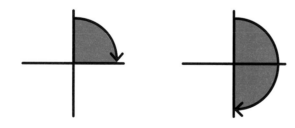

We will need some maths words.
Do you recognise any of these words?

quadrilateral　　　triangle　　　regular

irregular　　　interior angle　　　angle

acute　　　obtuse　　　reflect

right angle　　　symmetrical

isosceles　　　scalene　　　equilateral

line of symmetry　　　reflective symmetry

Can you identify the right angle?
Describe it to your partner.

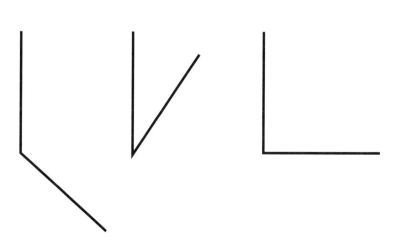

Identifying angles

Discover

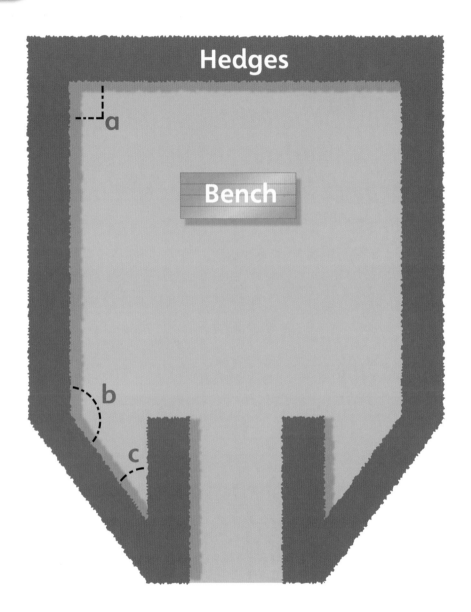

1 **a)** In which corners (**a**, **b** or **c**) of the garden can the bench be placed?

b) Explain what is the same and what is different between angles **a**, **b** and **c**.

Share

a) Angle **a** is the same size as the angle of the corners of the bench so it will fit neatly here.

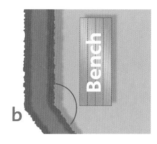

Angle **b** is larger than the angle of the corners of the bench so it can be placed here.

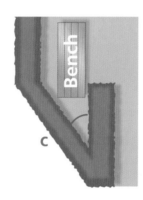

Angle **c** is smaller than the angle of the corners of the bench so it cannot be placed here.

b) All of the angles measure the turn between two walls of the garden.

Angle **a** is a quarter turn or a right angle.
Angle **b** is larger than a right angle.
Angle **c** is smaller than a right angle.

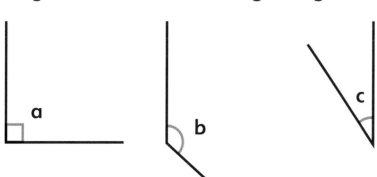

An angle between a quarter turn and a half turn is obtuse. An angle smaller than a quarter turn is acute.

Think together

1 Which corners will the bench fit in?

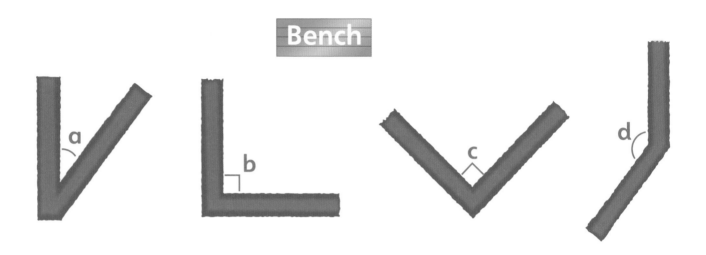

2 Can the bench below fit into the corner? How and why?

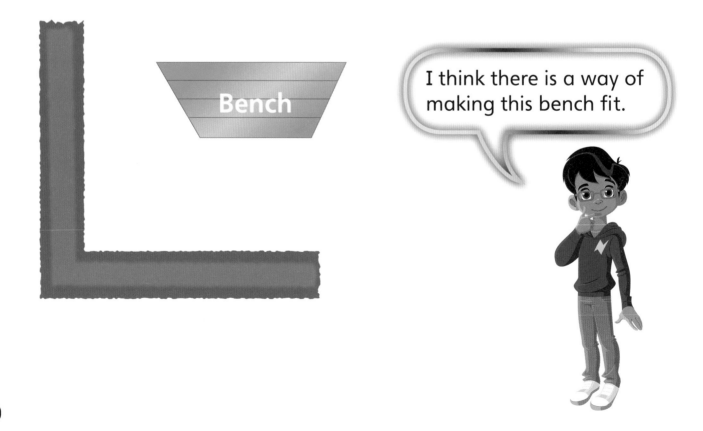

I think there is a way of making this bench fit.

 3 **a)** To which numbers could the clock hand point to show:

   i)   an acute turn?

   ii) a right angle turn?

   iii) an obtuse turn?

Acute is the name for an angle less than a right angle.

Obtuse is an angle greater than a right angle.

b) The clock hand has turned a right angle.

What number could it have been pointing to before it turned?

131

→ **Practice book 4C p93**

Comparing and ordering angles

Discover

Emma

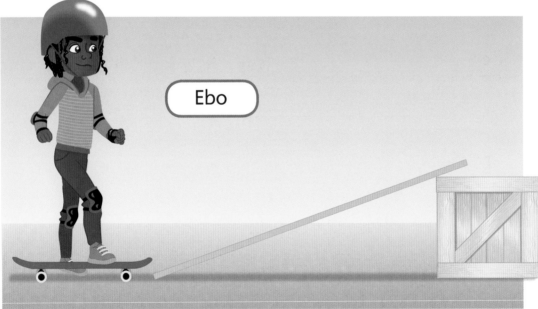

Ebo

1 **a)** Which ramp will allow the highest jump?

b) At what angle would each ramp stop working as a ramp?

132

Share

a) The children have set their ramps up at different angles. Emma's ramp has a greater angle than Ebo's ramp.

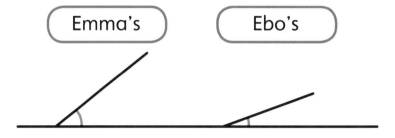

Emma's   Ebo's

As Emma's ramp is set to a greater angle than Ebo's, she would be able to jump the highest from her ramp.

> Both of these angles are smaller than a right angle. Remember, any angle smaller than a right angle is called an acute angle.

b) A ramp set at a right angle definitely would not be able to function as a ramp.

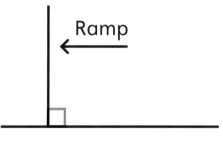

Ramp

> This will not work because the ramp is set at a right angle! I wonder if some acute angles also will not work.

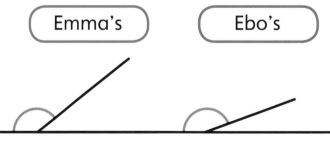

Emma's   Ebo's

> Remember, any angle which is larger than a right angle but less than a straight line is called an obtuse angle.

133

Think together

1 Sort these angles into groups by putting the letter of each angle in the correct column.

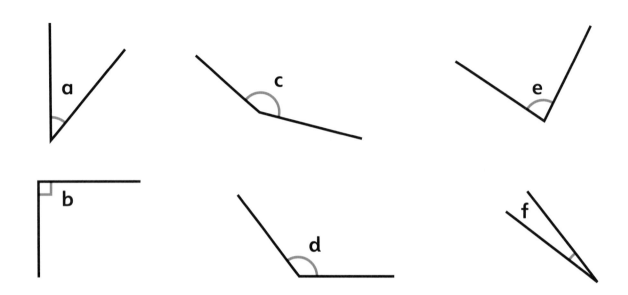

Acute	Right angle	Obtuse

2 Order the angles you have sorted from smallest to largest, writing them in a table like the one below.

Smallest				Largest

3 **a)** Sort the three shapes below. Complete the table by filling in all three columns for each category. One has been done for you.

A 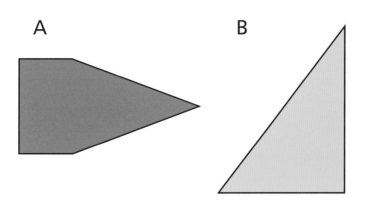   B   C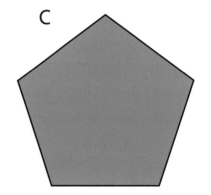

Fewest acute angles		Most acute angles
Fewest right angles		Most right angles
C		
Fewest obtuse angles		Most obtuse angles

b) Can you draw a four-sided shape with three acute angles and a right angle? Explain why or why not.

135

→ Practice book 4C p96

Identifying regular and irregular shapes

Discover

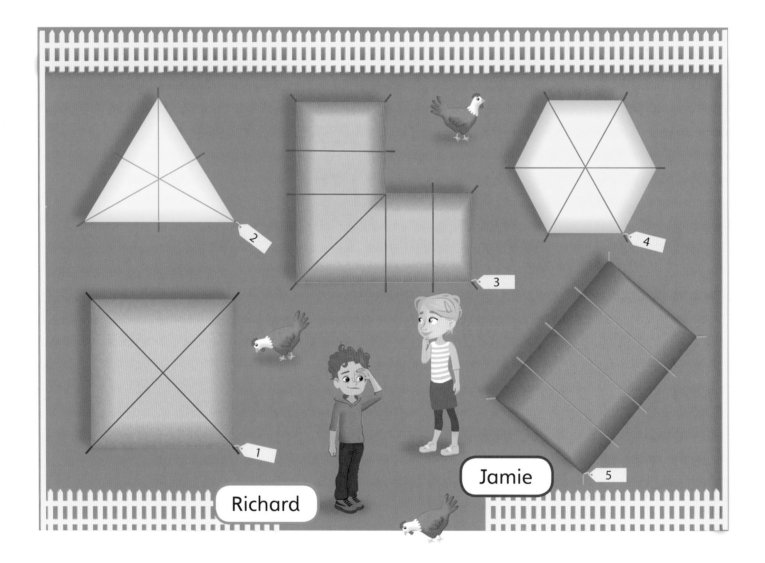

1 **a)** Richard remembers losing his favourite toy car near a hexagonal tent. Which could it have been?

b) Explain how the two hexagons are both similar and different.

136

Share

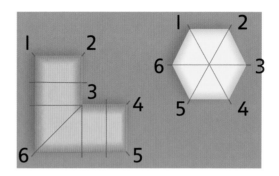

a) All hexagons have six sides and six vertices. There are two hexagonal tent outlines on the campsite.

Richard's toy car could be near either tent 3 or 4.

b)

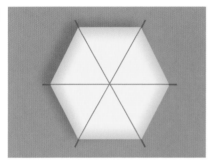

This hexagon has six sides that are all equal. It also has six **interior angles** that are all equal. This means it is a **regular** shape.

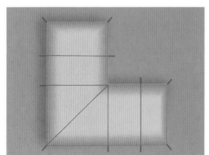

This hexagon has six sides as well but they are different lengths. It also has six interior angles but they are also different sizes. This means it is an **irregular** shape.

I know that interior angles are the angles inside a polygon.

A shape is regular only if all sides are the same length **and** all angles are the same size.

The two hexagons are similar as they both have six sides and six angles. They are different because their side lengths and interior angles are different sizes.

137

Think together

① Which of these shapes are irregular?

② Which shapes in this picture are regular and which are irregular? How do you know?

Alex has sorted some shapes. Has she sorted them correctly?

	Irregular	Regular
A four-sided shape	parallelogram	rectangle
Not a four-sided shape	hexagon	equilateral triangle and isosceles triangle

Name other shapes that could go in each section.

139

→ Practice book 4C p99

Classifying triangles

Discover

1 a) Ambika folds a square piece of paper in half diagonally and Lee folds a rectangular piece of paper in half diagonally. What shapes have they made?

b) How are the two different triangles similar and how are they different?

Share

a) When folded in half, both the square and the rectangular pieces of paper create types of triangles.

Ambika and Lee have made triangles.

b) Both triangles have a right angle.

The square makes a triangle that has two equal sides and two equal angles. This is called an **isosceles** triangle.

The rectangle makes a triangle that has three unequal sides and three unequal angles. This is called a **scalene** triangle.

There is another type of triangle. A triangle that has three equal sides and three equal angles is called an **equilateral** triangle.

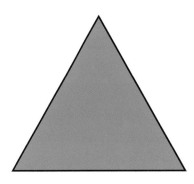

141

Think together

1. Which of these triangles is a scalene triangle?

A   B   C

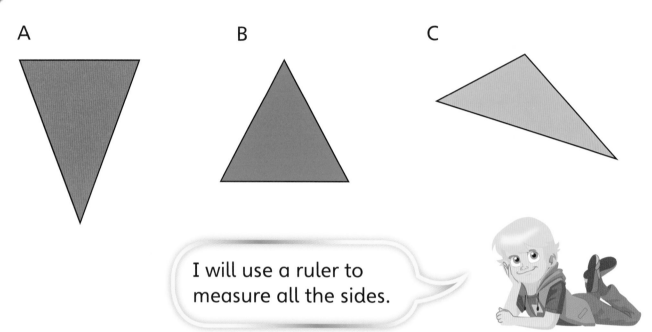

I will use a ruler to measure all the sides.

2. Which of these isosceles triangles have 3 acute angles?

A   B   C   D

E

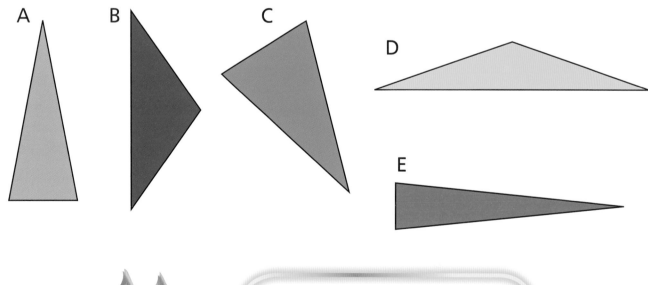

Remember, an acute angle is less than a quarter turn.

3 **a)** How many different triangles can you make on a 3×3 geoboard?

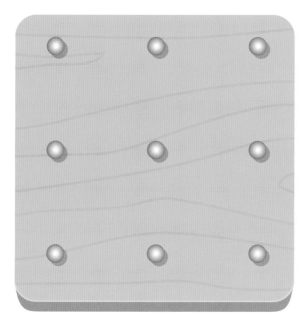

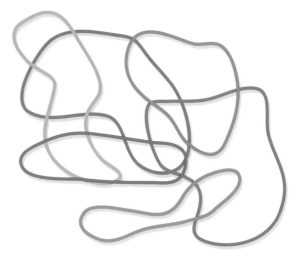

b) Have you found them all? How do you know?

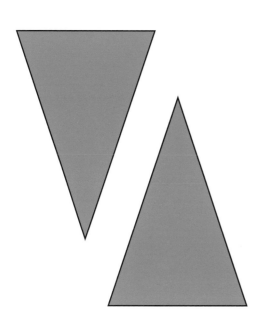

I wonder whether these triangles are different. Perhaps they are the same but rotated differently.

143

Classifying and comparing quadrilaterals

Discover

Olivia

1 **a)** Olivia is making shapes with geostrips. What is the same and what is different about the shapes she has made?

b) What shape is a regular quadrilateral?

Share

a) Quadrilaterals can have different lengths and different angles from each other.

> I remember that a polygon with four sides is called a quadrilateral.

Olivia's shapes all have four sides but each has different angles.

b) A quadrilateral with four equal sides is called a rhombus. The interior angles of a rhombus may be different but its sides are all the same length.

Rhombuses

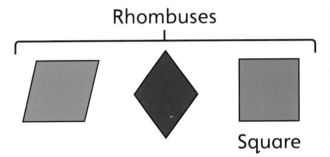

Square

A square is the only regular quadrilateral and is a special type of rhombus. It has four equal sides and four equal angles.

> I remember that only one thing needs to be different for a shape to be irregular.

Regular	Irregular
All sides are equal.	
All interior angles are equal.	Interior angles and/or sides are unequal.

Think together

1 A parallelogram is a quadrilateral which has two pairs of parallel sides. Identify all the parallelograms.

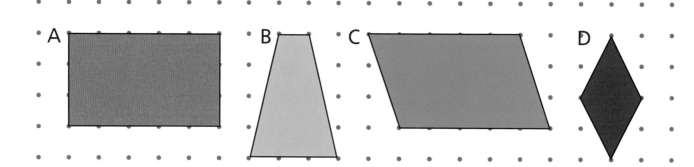

How do you know?

Remember, parallel lines are two lines that are always the same distance apart and never touch.

2 A trapezium has one pair of parallel sides. The other pair of sides can be the same length or different lengths.

Draw a different trapezium to the one pictured here. Use squared paper to help you.

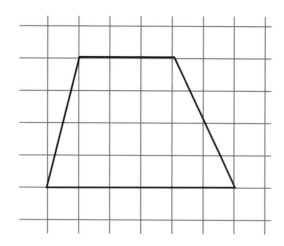

I wonder if a parallelogram is a kind of trapezium.

3 **a)** By drawing lines between the points like those below, what quadrilaterals can you create?

CHALLENGE

```
•   •   •   •

•   •   •   •

•   •   •   •

•   •   •   •
```

b) Organise your shapes into a sorting diagram like this.

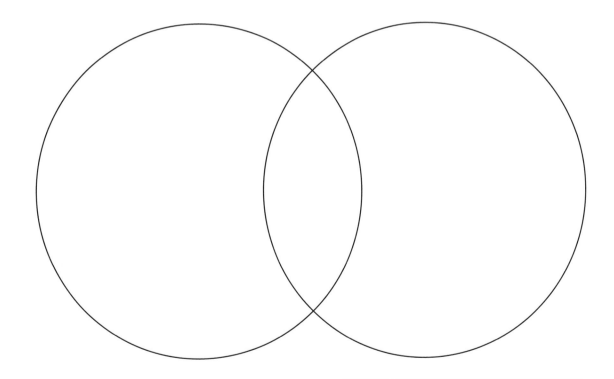

Contains a right angle

Sides the same length

147

→ Practice book 4C p105

Deducing facts about shapes

Discover

I can make an irregular hexagon!

Bella

1 a) Bella has made a shape by overlapping two pieces of square paper. Explain why Bella's shape cannot be a regular hexagon.

What other shapes could Bella make?

b) What shape could Bella make with the largest number of corners?

Share

a) The shape Bella has made cannot be a regular hexagon as the sides are not equal and the angles are not equal.

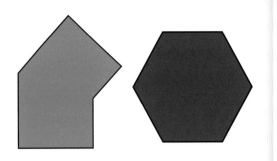

Regular shapes have equal length sides and equal angles.

Bella could use her squares of paper to create shapes such as these.

I think there are more shapes she could make.

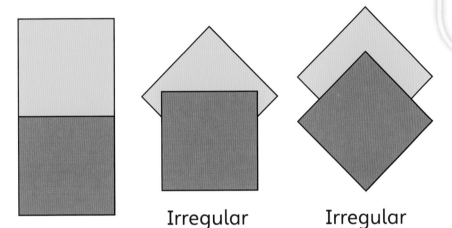

Rectangle

Irregular heptagon

Irregular octagon

b) To make the shape with the largest number of corners, Bella should arrange the two squares like this:

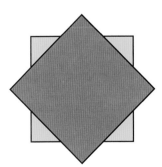

This shape is called a hexadecagon.

Think together

1 Raj makes this shape with two different quadrilateral pieces of paper.

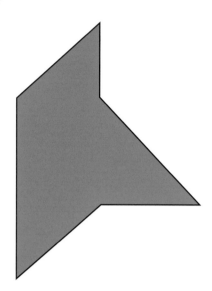

What shapes could they have been?

2 Ruby has five equilateral triangles. She joins them along their edges to make different shapes.

Ruby has made a rhombus using two of the triangles.

What different shapes can she make? (She does not have to use them all.)

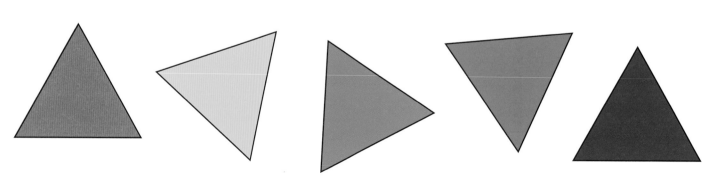

Prove your ideas.

3 **a)** Jamilla has made a pentagon by shading the area where two square pieces of paper overlap. What other shapes could Jamilla make in this way?

Jamilla

b) Can she make all the different types of quadrilateral?

Use the table to help you.

Quadrilateral	Can it be made?
square	
rectangle	
rhombus	
trapezium	
kite	
arrowhead	

I wonder if she can make a regular pentagon.

151

→ **Practice book 4C p108**

Lines of symmetry inside a shape

Discover

I can find two ways to fold this square in half.

Max

1 **a)** Is Max correct? Has he found all the ways of folding the square in half?

b) How many lines of symmetry are there in an equilateral triangle?

Share

a)

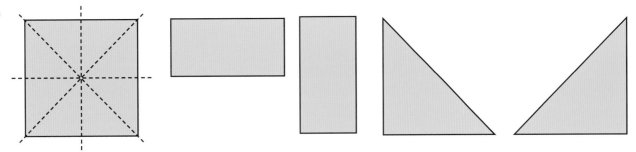

Max is incorrect. There are four lines of symmetry inside a square.
So there are four ways of folding the square.

b)

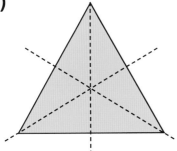 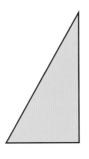 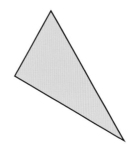 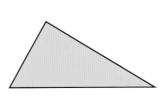

In an equilateral triangle, there are three lines of symmetry.

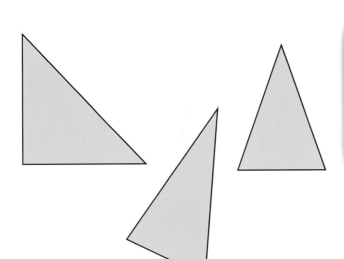

I wonder if other types of triangle have three lines of reflective symmetry too. This means a mirror held on that line will show the whole shape exactly.

Think together

1 Dominic says he has found a line of symmetry in this rectangle. Is he correct? Explain your reasoning.

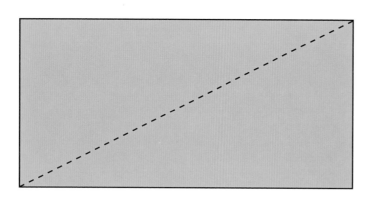

I will try folding a rectangular piece of paper to check.

2 How many lines of symmetry do these two hexagons have?

A

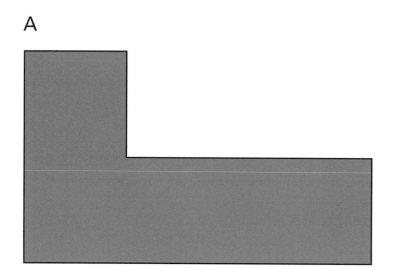

B

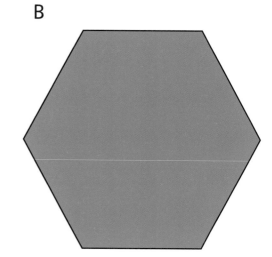

3 Identify the lines of symmetry in these shapes.

CHALLENGE

I will use a mirror to check.

I think some of these shapes do not have any lines of symmetry.

→ **Practice book 4C p111**

Lines of symmetry outside a shape

Discover

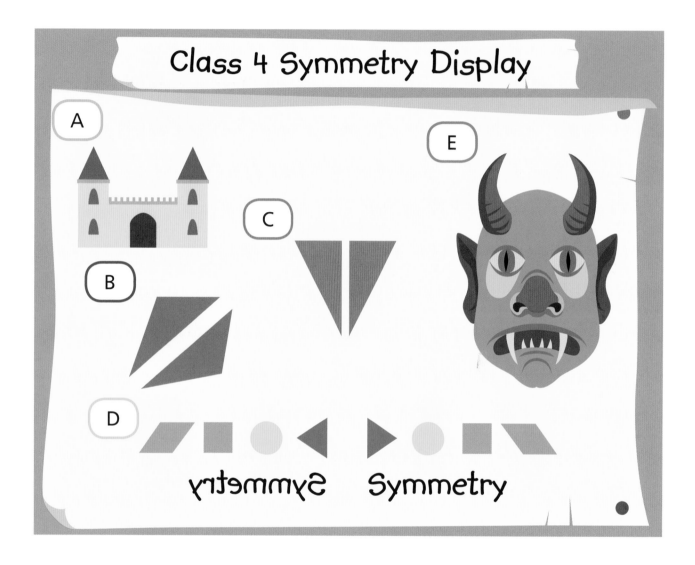

I **a)** How many different lines of symmetry can you see?

b) What do you notice about the monster picture?

Share

a) Shapes A, B and C have one line of symmetry each.

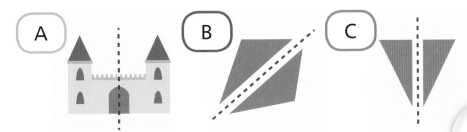

A has a vertical line of symmetry.
B has a diagonal line of symmetry.
C has a vertical line of symmetry.

I think there might be some symmetry inside each shape as well.

D also has a vertical line of symmetry. The individual shapes in D also have lines of symmetry.

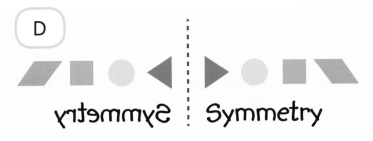

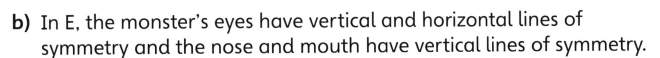

ʏɿɈemmʏƧ : Symmetry

b) In E, the monster's eyes have vertical and horizontal lines of symmetry and the nose and mouth have vertical lines of symmetry.

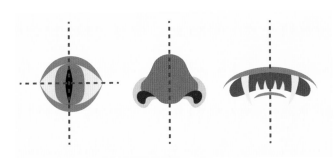

E

The whole face has a vertical line of symmetry.

Think together

1 Spot the lines of symmetry in these monsters.

A   B   C

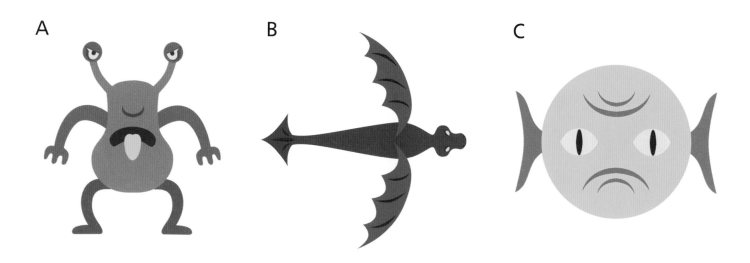

2 Where is the line of symmetry in this monster?

a) What lines of symmetry can you find in these patterns?

A

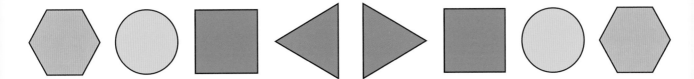

B

> I can find vertical lines of symmetry but I think there might be more.

b) Make your own symmetrical border pattern using shapes or drawings.

159

Completing a symmetric figure

Discover

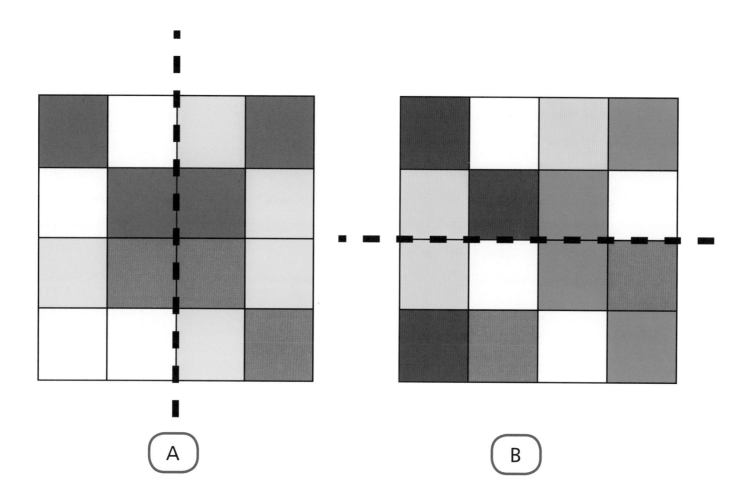

A

B

1 **a)** Zac needs to complete symmetric design A.

What coloured tiles does he need and where should he place them?

b) How would Zac complete design B to make it symmetric?

Share

a) To complete design A, Zac needs one red and three yellow tiles.

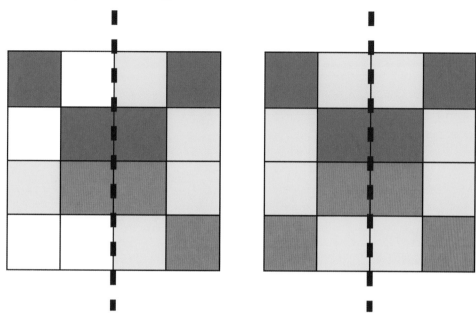

b) To make design B symmetric, Zac needs one purple, one orange, and two red tiles.

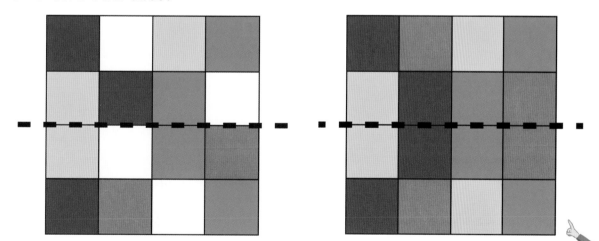

I notice design A has a vertical line of symmetry while design B has a horizontal line of symmetry.

Think together

1 What coloured tiles are needed to complete this symmetric design?

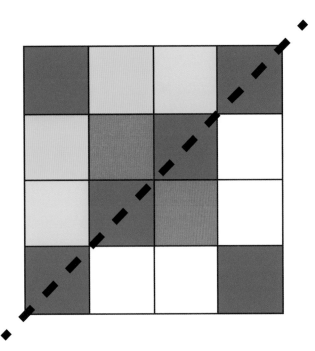

2 Identify all the lines of symmetry in this design.

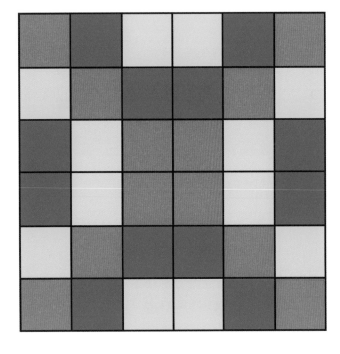

I wonder whether there is a diagonal line of symmetry.

3 Two tiles are missing from this design. Which two tiles are they and where do they go?

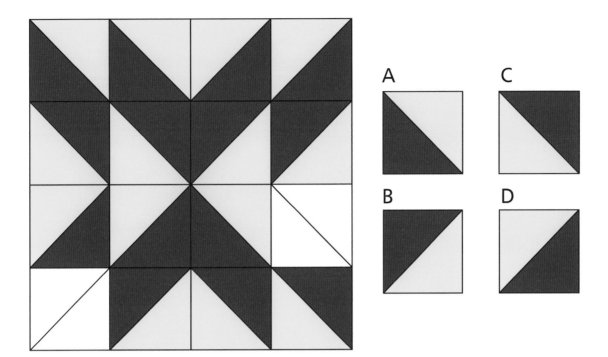

4 In his class, Mr Lopez has eleven identical oblong desks. He wants to arrange them in a symmetric pattern with both a vertical and a horizontal line of symmetry.

CHALLENGE

How could he arrange the desks?

Use eleven rectangular pieces of paper to test out your ideas.

An oblong rectangle is a rectangle that has two longer sides and two shorter sides.

163

→ Practice book 4C p117

Completing a symmetric shape

Discover

Isla

Isla is building a symmetric, octagonal pen for her chickens.
She has used five pieces of fence so far.

1 **a)** She uses five more lengths of fence.

What does her chicken pen look like?

How many lines of symmetry does it have?

b) Could she complete the symmetric pattern with less than five pieces of fence?

164

Share

a) Isla's chicken pen would look like this once it has been completed with five more pieces of fence.

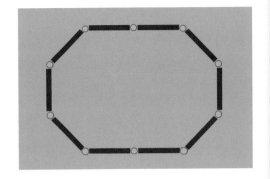

This shape has two lines of symmetry.

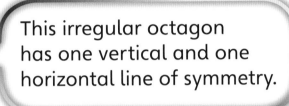

This irregular octagon has one vertical and one horizontal line of symmetry.

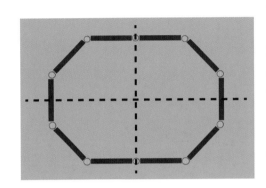

b) Isla could complete a symmetric, octagonal pen by using only three more pieces of fence. This is what the pen would look like.

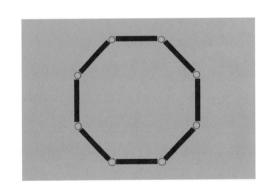

This regular octagon has 8 lines of symmetry.

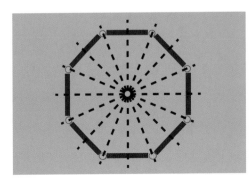

165

Think together

1 Complete the symmetric figures using lolly sticks.

a)

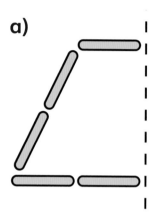

b)

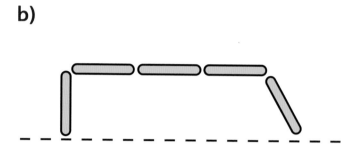

2 Complete these symmetric shapes made of lolly sticks.

a)

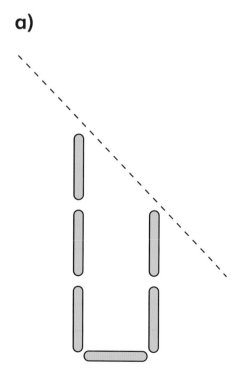

b)

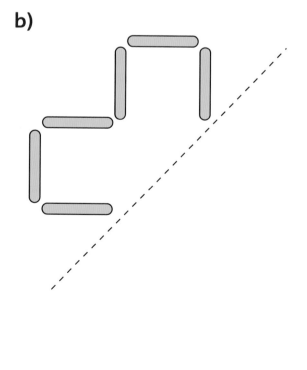

3 Kate makes three conjectures about symmetric shapes.

Prove which are true and which are false.

Use squared paper to help you.

I can draw a quadrilateral that when reflected along one side will create a pentagon.

If half my shape has three sides then the reflected shape must be a hexagon.

If I reflect a shape the number of sides always doubles.

Kate

167

End of unit check

1 Identify the irregular quadrilateral.

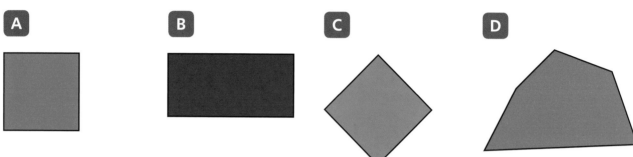

2 Which set of shapes correctly completes the symmetric pattern?

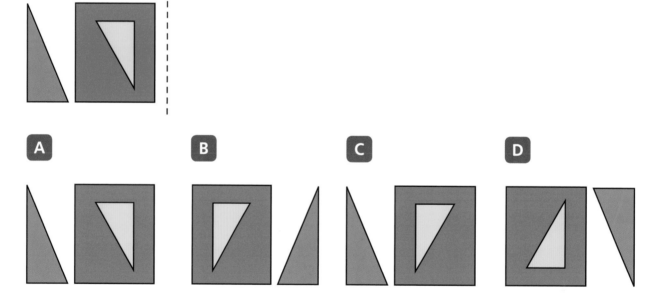

3 Identify the isosceles triangle.

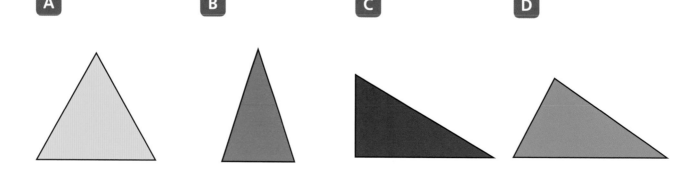

4 Identify the shape which has more than 3 obtuse angles.

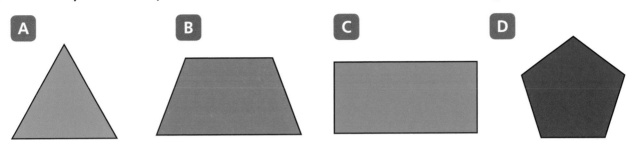

5 Identify the shape with exactly 2 lines of symmetry.

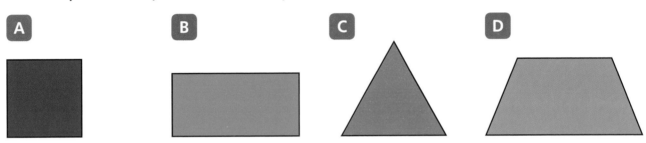

6 This square has been divided into four triangles **A**, **B**, **C** and **D**.

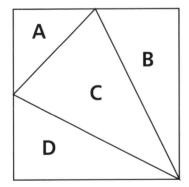

a) Write the letters of all the triangles that have a **right angle**.

b) Write the letters of all the triangles that have **two equal sides**.

169

→ Practice book 4C p123

Unit 16
Geometry – position and direction

In this unit we will …

- ⚡ Use numbers to say where things are on a grid
- ⚡ Plot points on a grid
- ⚡ Use our knowledge of shapes to complete diagrams
- ⚡ Describe movements on a grid

Point A is '2 across and 1 up'. Where is Point B?

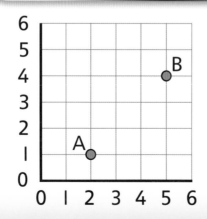

We will need some maths words. Which ones go together?

position   horizontal   vertical

up   down   left   right

coordinate   square   rectangle

plot   vertex   vertices

point   grid

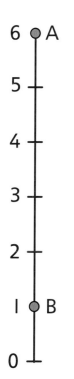

You will need to know how to find numbers on a number line. What are the numbers marked with letters?

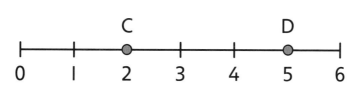

Describing position ❶

Discover

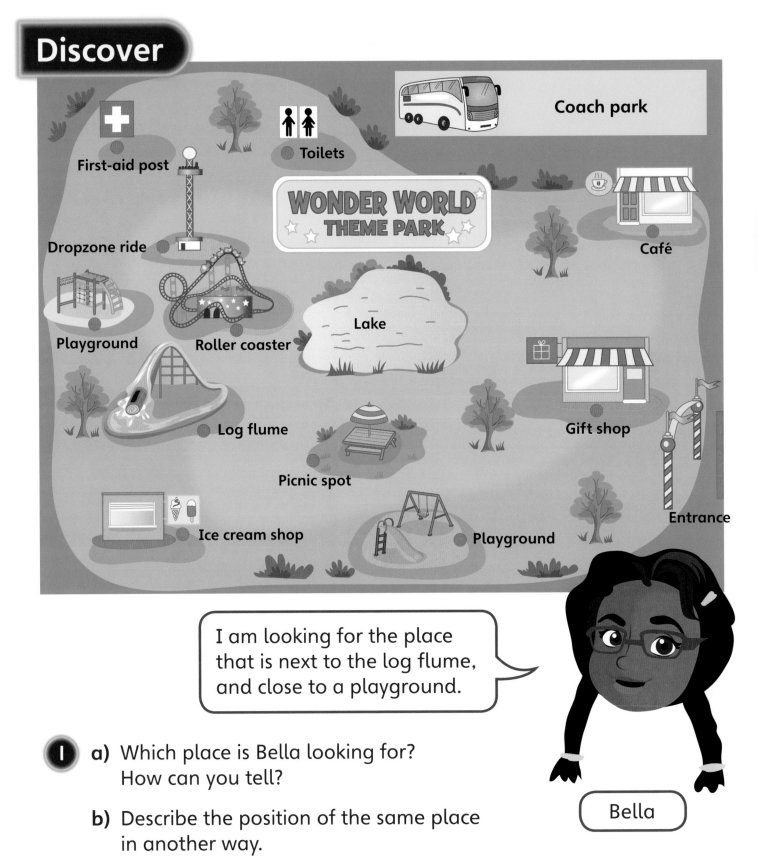

> I am looking for the place that is next to the log flume, and close to a playground.

Bella

❶ **a)** Which place is Bella looking for? How can you tell?

b) Describe the position of the same place in another way.

172

Share

a) The roller coaster, the picnic spot and the ice cream shop are all next to the log flume.

I need to use both pieces of information. Only one place is next to the log flume **and** close to a playground.

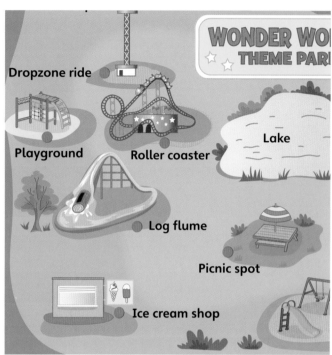

Bella is looking for the roller coaster.

b) The position of the roller coaster can be described in lots of different ways.

I will say that the roller coaster is between the playground and the lake.

I wonder if it is exactly half-way.

The roller coaster is half-way between the log flume and the dropzone ride.

Think together

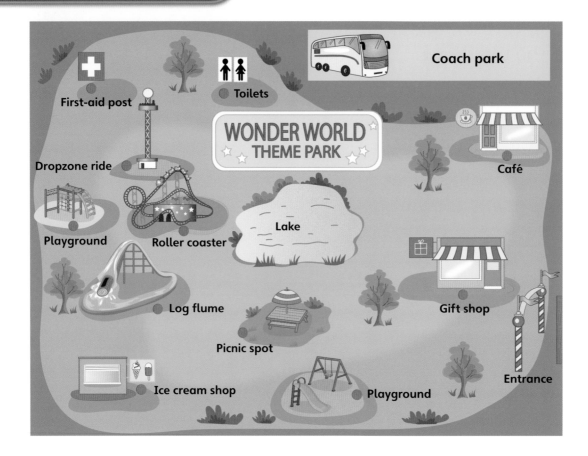

1. Identify each of these places from its description.

   a) The place near the top of the map, close to the coach park.

   b) The feature in the centre of the map.

   c) The closest place to the entrance.

   d) The closest place to the lake.

2. Describe the positions of these places. There may be more than one way to describe each one.

   a) The ice cream shop   c) The dropzone ride

   b) The café   d) The first aid post

3 Here is another version of the map of the theme park.

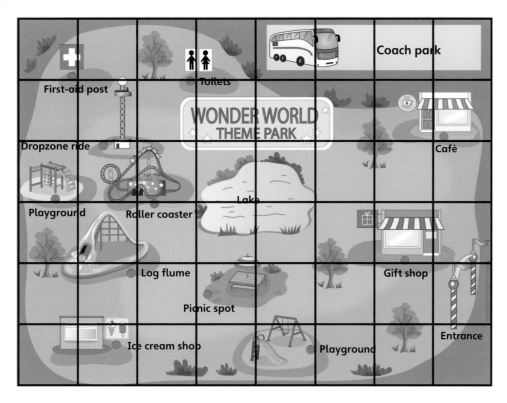

Use this version of the map to find each of these places from its description.

a) This place is half-way between the roller coaster and the ice cream shop.

b) This place is two spaces to the right of the first aid post.

c) This place is seven spaces across from the left edge of the map, and three spaces up from the bottom.

Do the squares on the map (the **grid**) make it easier to say where things are? Why?

175

Describing position ❷

Discover

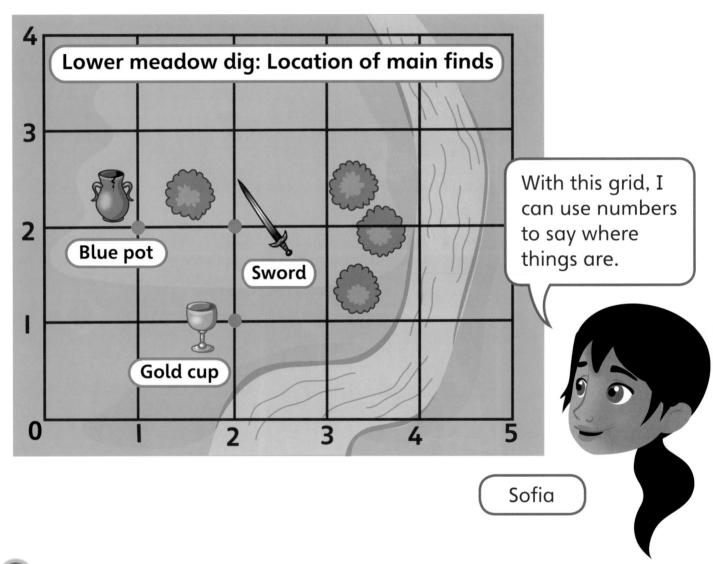

Lower meadow dig: Location of main finds

Blue pot

Sword

Gold cup

With this grid, I can use numbers to say where things are.

Sofia

1 **a)** Which object was found at position (2,2)?

b) What was found at position (2,1)?

Share

a)

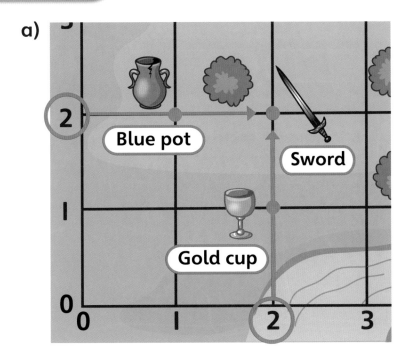

The sword was found at position (2,2).

b)

I think the blue pot is at (2,1), as it is 2 up and 1 across.

I think the gold cup is at (2,1) as it is 2 across and 1 up.

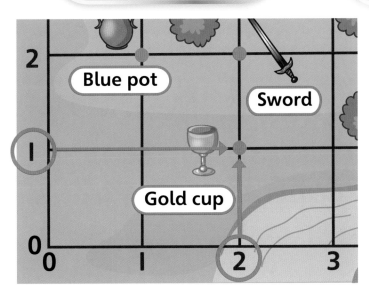

We always put the number across first, so (2,1) means 2 along and 1 up. (2,1) are called the **coordinates** of the point.

The gold cup was found at position (2,1).

Think together

1 Sofia marked the positions of some other objects on the map.

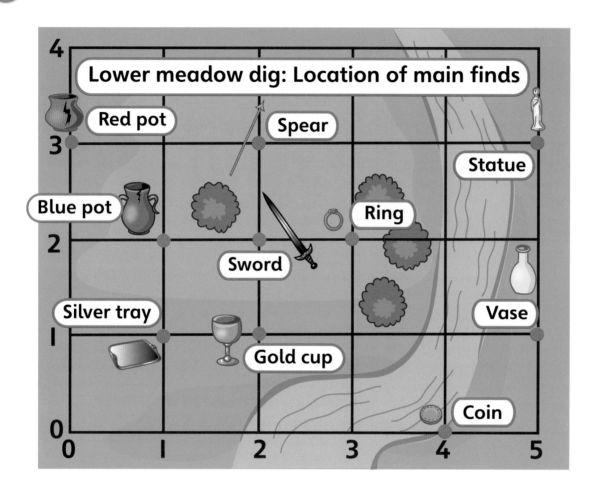

a) What is located at (1,2)?

b) What is located at (5,3)?

c) What is at the position with coordinates (2,3)?

2 **a)** Give the coordinates of the silver tray.

b) Where were these objects found?

    i) The red pot

    ii) The coin

    iii) The vase

3 A dog walker found an old silver pin in the middle of the trees. Which of these could **not** be the position where the pin was found?

A (2,2)

B (3,2)

C (2,3)

> I need to remember to find the first coordinate along the horizontal line and the second coordinate upwards from there.

179

→ Practice book 4C p129

Drawing on a grid

Discover

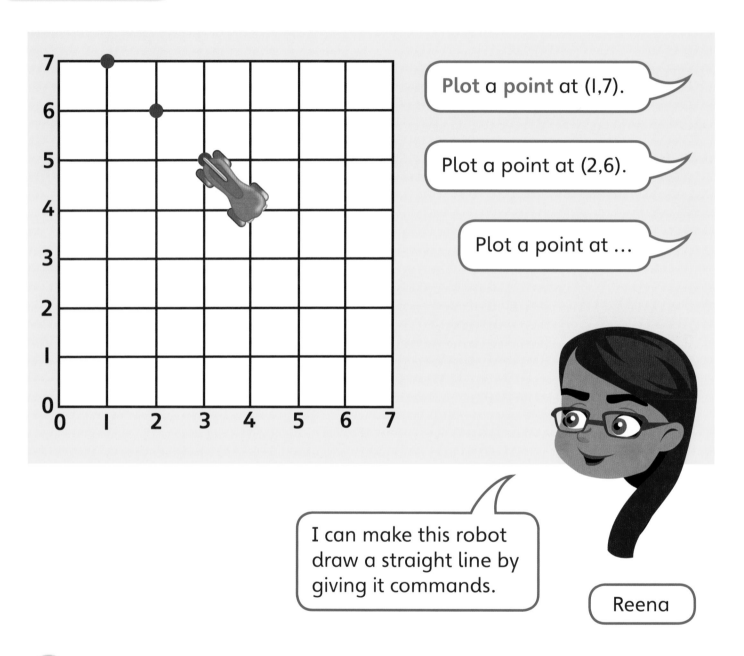

Plot a point at (1,7).

Plot a point at (2,6).

Plot a point at ...

I can make this robot draw a straight line by giving it commands.

Reena

1 a) What command did Reena use to plot the third dot?

b) What points should Reena plot to continue the dots in a straight line?

Share

a) The command Reena used to plot the third dot is:
Plot a point at (3,5).

I am going to start from zero. I will count across (horizontally), then up (vertically) to find the coordinates.

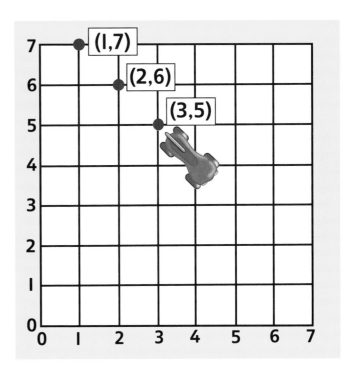

b)

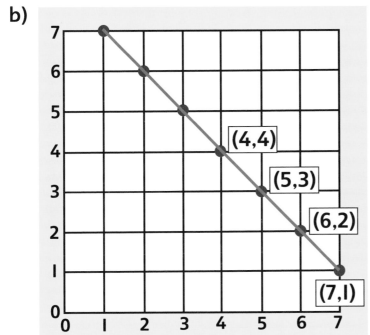

I can draw a straight line through the dots to find the new points.

Reena should plot the points (4,4), (5,3), (6,2) and (7,1) to continue the dots in a straight line.

181

Think together

1 Plot these points on a grid.

What pattern do the points make?

(5,7), (4,6), (3,5), (2,4), (1,3), (0,2)

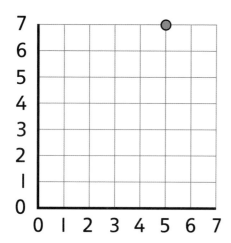

2 a) What are the coordinates of these points?

b) Plot the points that continue the same line.

List their coordinates.

Look at the list of coordinates. Could you have predicted what they were without plotting all the points?

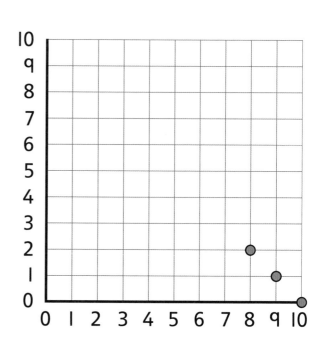

3) Emma used a robot to plot the points on the outline of a capital 'E'.

Plot a point at (0,4).

Plot a point at (3,4).

Emma

What were the rest of the commands that she used?

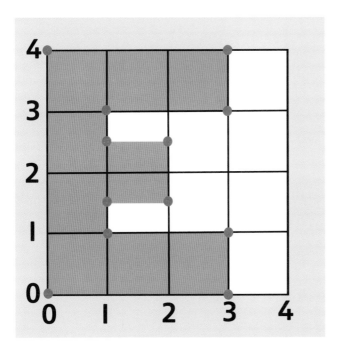

Some of the coordinates are not whole numbers. I will need to use fractions.

183

Reasoning on a grid

Discover

Move to (1,4).

Draw a line to (1,1).

Draw a line to (4,1).

I can make this robot draw lines to make a square.

Richard

1 **a)** What command should Richard give next?

b) What is the final command that is needed to finish the square?

Share

I will shade the square to find where the missing corner is.

a)

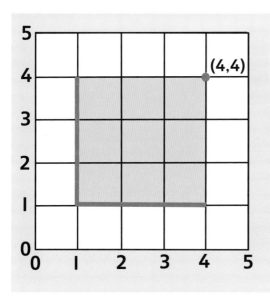

The next command Richard should give is: Draw a line to (4,4).

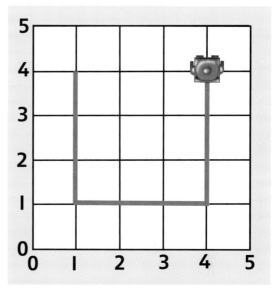

b)

A square has four sides, so you need to go back to the starting point to finish it.

The final command that is needed to finish the square is: Draw a line to (1,4).

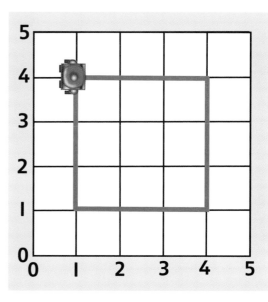

Think together

① Zeb has plotted points at three of the corners of a rectangle.

What are the coordinates of the final corner?

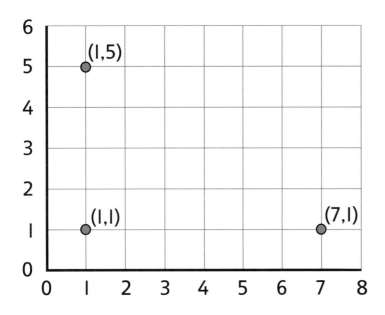

② The two points on this grid are two corners of a square. The whole square fits inside the grid.

What are the coordinates of the other two corners?

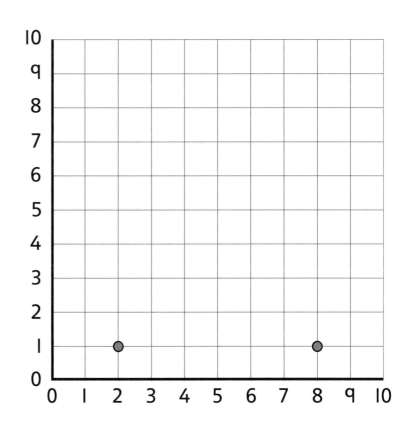

186

3 The two points on this grid are two corners of a square.

What are the coordinates of the other two corners? (There is more than one answer!)

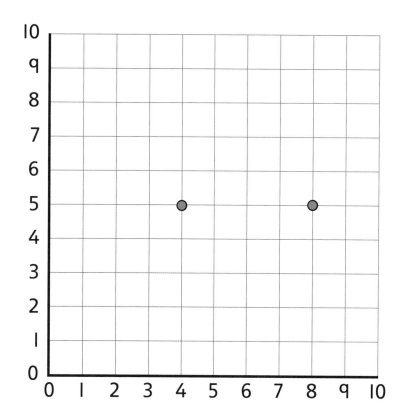

4 The blue shape is part of a shape with one line of symmetry.

What are the missing coordinates of the vertices of the shape?

CHALLENGE

I can remember how to do this. Each vertex is the same distance on the other side of the line of symmetry.

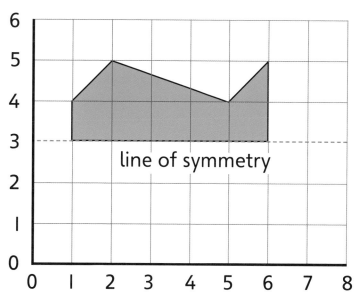

line of symmetry

187

→ **Practice book 4C p135**

Moving on a grid

Discover

I am exploring a new site with a drone. There is something else I want to have a look at.

Go 2 right and 2 up.

Sofia

1 **a)** What feature does Sofia want to look at?

b) Later, the drone was at the tower and Sofia told it to move 5 left and 2 up. Where did she send the drone to?

Share

a) Sofia wants to look at the jetty.

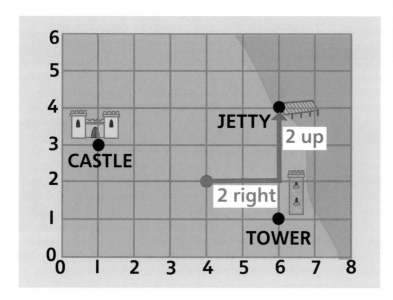

I will draw the lines on the grid to show the drone going 2 right and 2 up.

b) The drone starts at the tower for this movement.

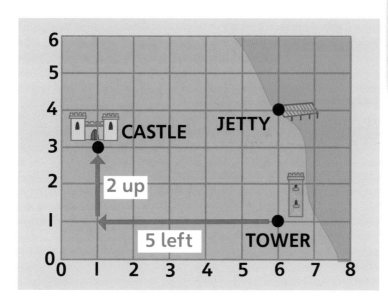

I wonder whether I could work out where the drone would go without drawing on the map.

Sofia sent the drone to the castle.

Think together

1 These commands will take the drone to all of the places marked on the map in turn.

What order will the drone visit the places in?

- 1 left, 3 up

- 4 right, 3 down

- 1 left, 3 up

- 4 down

- 5 left, 2 up

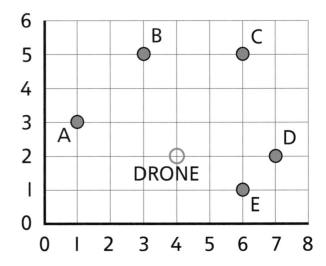

2 The map shows the position of three towns.

The journey from P to Q is '3 right, 1 up'. What journeys do these instructions describe?

a) 3 left, 1 down

b) 4 right, 3 down

c) 4 left, 3 up

d) 1 right, 4 down

e) 1 left, 4 up

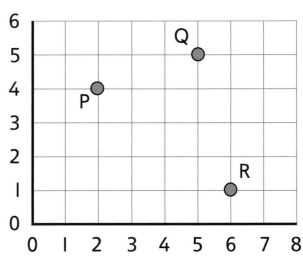

③ The orange rectangle slides across the grid so that corner A moves from (1,1) to (7,4).

Where do the three other corners of the rectangle move to?

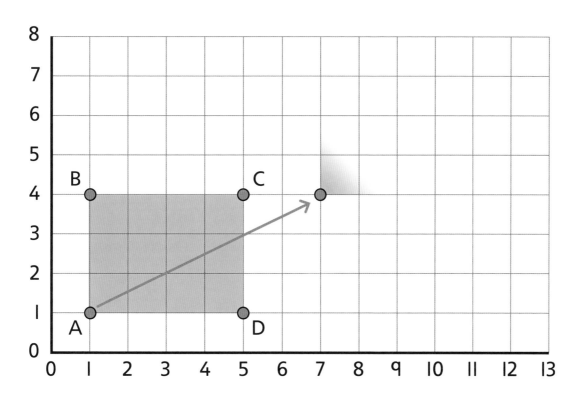

I will work out where each corner has moved to in turn.

I think there is another way. I will try to draw the rectangle in its new position.

191

→ Practice book 4C p138

Describing a movement on a grid

Discover

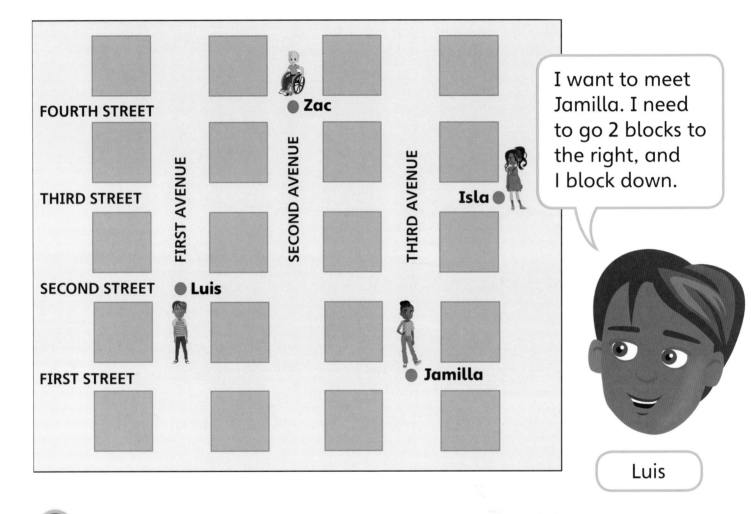

1 a) Luis could write his journey to Jamilla as '2 right, 1 down'.

   If Jamilla went to Luis instead, how could she write her journey?

b) Zac wants to meet Isla. He is not sure which of these is the correct journey:

   • 2 right and then 1 down

   • 1 down and then 2 right.

   Which is correct?

Share

a)

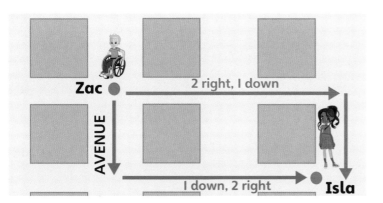

I think that Jamilla's journey is in the opposite direction to Luis's. So she will go left instead of right, and up instead of down.

Jamilla could write her journey as '2 left, I up'.

b)

I am going to draw both journeys on the grid and see where Zac finishes.

It is the same journey whether you do the down part first, or the right part. I wonder why.

The journeys are the same: both are correct.

Think together

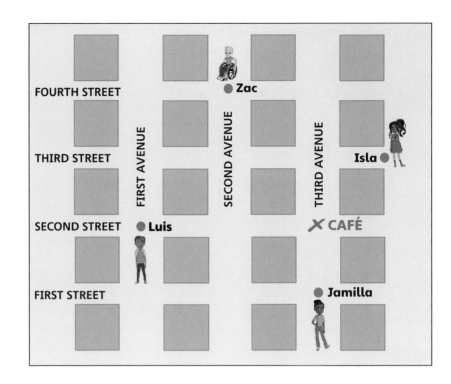

1. The four friends decide that they will all meet at a café at the point marked with an X.

a) Describe Zac's journey.

Zac's journey is ⬚ _____ , ⬚ _____

b)

Who is right? Explain your answer.

c) Describe Luis's journey in two ways.

d) Describe Jamilla's journey.

2 The journey from A to B can be written as '5 left, 2 up'.

Write the other journeys.

A to B: 5 left, 2 up   B to A

A to C   C to A

B to C   C to B

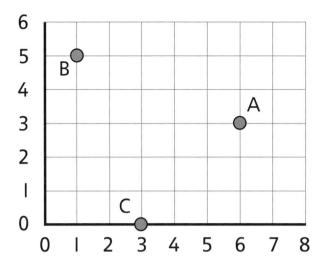

3 Describe these journeys.

a) The blue rectangle moves to rectangle A.

b) The blue rectangle moves to rectangle B.

c) The blue rectangle moves to rectangle C.

CHALLENGE

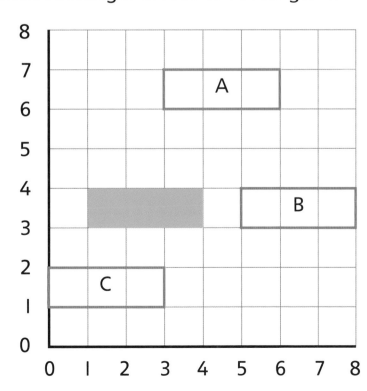

195

→ **Practice book 4C p141**

End of unit check

1 Which point has been plotted in the wrong position?

   A Point Q

   B Point R

   C Point S

   D Point T

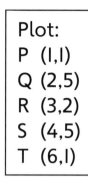

Plot:
P (1,1)
Q (2,5)
R (3,2)
S (4,5)
T (6,1)

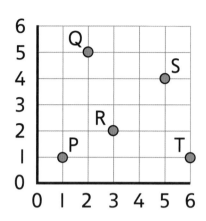

2 Points E and F are two of the corners of a square.

Which of these points could not be another corner of the same square?

   A Point A

   B Point B

   C Point C

   D Point D

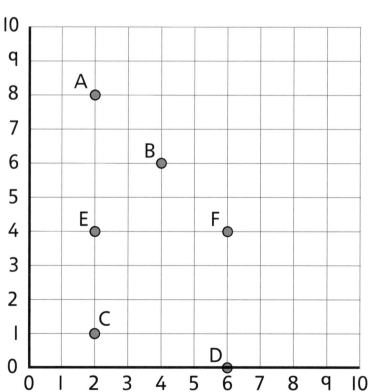

Use this grid for questions 3 to 5.

3 Which point would these instructions take you to?

Start at point G. Move 3 right, I down.

A Point J

B Point K

C Point H

D Point M

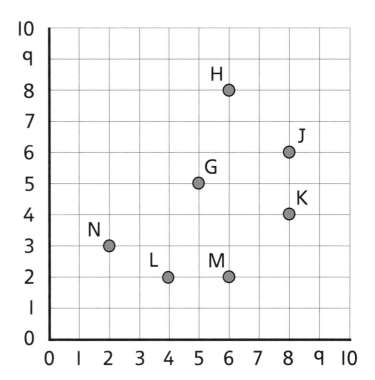

4 Which instructions describe the journey from G to N?

A 4 left, 3 down

B 3 left, 2 down

C 3 left, 4 down

D 2 left, 3 down

5 The journey 'I left, 3 down' finished at point G. Where did it start?

A Point H

B Point J

C Point L

D Point M

6 Draw the quadrilateral with vertices at (4,8), (7,5), (7,0) and (2,5) on a grid.

Which point could you move to change the quadrilateral to a square? What are the coordinates of the new point?

197

→ Practice book 4C p144

Holiday fun

Here are some ideas you can try at home.

Towers

Build towers using playing cards, trading cards or cards from a board game. Investigate different techniques and remember to show determination. You will need a steady hand, some problem-solving skills and the mental strength not to give up too easily!

If you visit the beach or have some space in your garden then have a go at building towers from pebbles. Use small flat pebbles, so no one hurts their toes if there is a sudden collapse!

Puzzle games

Research some different puzzle games. Can you become an expert in noughts and crosses by working out the best starting positions? Or the best tactics if your opponent goes first? What about if you play on a 4 × 4 grid?

With an adult, research the rules of some of these other simple but fun puzzle games that get your brain thinking: Nim, Squares, Hex …

You might be able to make a board to play each game on.

Olympic Games

Set up an Olympic Games competition for your family. Invent challenges such as standing long jump, throwing accuracy, hopping height or skipping speed. If it is too rainy, then invent some indoor challenges such as: who can write their name the most times in 1 minute, or who can say the alphabet quickest.

Keep records of your family world records, and work out how to measure the different events as accurately as possible. How will you carefully measure the distance, time or number of skips?

Mathematical art

Use your mathematical imagination to create some intricate art designs. You could investigate the different kinds of stars you can draw by drawing lines from the corners of different 2D shapes, or the different kinds of spirals you can design using 100 cm of string. What about using different lengths of coloured wool to make a mathematical design? You could use different shapes and angles to create interesting patterns.

What have we learnt?

Can you do all these things?

- ⚡ Order decimals
- ⚡ Round money to the nearest pound
- ⚡ Write time in different ways
- ⚡ Read data from line graphs
- ⚡ Identify lines of symmetry
- ⚡ Plot points on a grid

Some of it was difficult, but we did not give up!

Now you are ready for the next books!